BUTTERFLY UNFOLDED

A HEARTFELT NARRATIVE OF SELF-DISCOVERY

ANUSHRI RAMESH

"For every soul seeking light in their journey, this book is my heart reaching out to yours."

Contents

Contents

Foreword

In *Butterfly Unfolded*, Anushri Ramesh explores the profound interconnectedness of the mind, body, heart, and spirit, revealing how personal well-being shapes and mirrors the collective health of humanity.

Blending scientific insights with spiritual wisdom, this transformative guide unpacks:

- The interconnected systems of health and their impact on personal and global harmony.
- Practical strategies for achieving balance and self-awareness in a fragmented world.
- The role of individual growth in fostering a healthier, more connected humanity.

Drawing from her journey as a scientist, psychologist, and mother, Anushri offers an authentic and compassionate perspective on living with purpose and alignment.

Step into self-discovery, embrace holistic health and transform your connection with the world.

Anushri Ramesh is an author, psychologist, and mother of two with an unwavering passion for storytelling. With a background in science and a heart deeply rooted in human connection, Anushri brings a unique blend of logic and empathy to her work. After choosing to leave her PhD in nano-biotechnology to embrace family, she embarked on a journey that led her to discover the profound joy and challenges of motherhood, healing, and personal growth.

Her writing reflects her belief that every setback is a stepping stone to something greater, and every transformation is worth celebrating, no matter how small.

Her debut book, "Butterfly Unfolded," is a testament to the resilience of the human spirit and the magic of metamorphosis.

৪৩

PREFACE

Transformation is the essence of life. Like the caterpillar that retreats into its cocoon, unaware of the metamorphosis it is about to undergo, we often find ourselves in life's cocoons enclosed by doubt, pain, love, or longing. But when the time is right, we emerge. Stronger. Lighter. More radiant than we ever imagined. *Butterfly Unfolded* is my attempt to capture this universal journey of transformation and to celebrate the strength that lies in vulnerability and the beauty that emerges from chaos.

This book is deeply personal yet profoundly universal. It's an amalgamation of my experiences as a mother, a wife, a psychologist, and above all, a woman constantly seeking growth. I have drawn from the myriad roles I have played the scientist who left the lab, the woman who rebuilt her identity post-motherhood, the friend who healed from betrayal, and the dreamer who never stopped chasing aspirations. Each chapter reflects these phases, woven together to form a tapestry of resilience and hope.

When I decided to pen this book, I was guided by two emotions: the desire to share my journey and the hope that my words would resonate with someone navigating their cocoon. I have always believed that stories connect us in ways no other medium can. They remind us that we are not alone, that our struggles are shared, and that our triumphs, no matter how small, are worth celebrating.

The title, *Butterfly Unfolded*, is a metaphor that perfectly encapsulates my journey and, I believe, the journeys of many others. The butterfly's wings, delicate yet powerful, symbolize the duality of life—its fragility and its strength. To unfold is not merely to emerge but to expand, to embrace one's true self unapologetically.

As you turn the pages, you will find stories of self-discovery, essays on healing, and reflections on love and identity. Some narratives will take you to moments of joy, while others might lead you into shadows I have learned to embrace. Each word is written with raw honesty, in the hope that it encourages you to reflect on your own metamorphosis.

I am immensely grateful to those who have been part of my journey, my family, who anchors me; my husband, whose unwavering support has been my cocoon's strength; my children, who remind me daily of life's wonder; and the readers, like you, who allow my words to come alive.

Butterfly Unfolded is not just a book. It is an invitation to look within, to embrace your cocoon, and to celebrate your wings. May these pages inspire you to honour your own transformations, for it is in unfolding that we truly soar.

With love and gratitude,

Anushri Ramesh

Acknowledgements

This book would not have been possible without my family's unwavering support and love.

To my Pappa, M. Arunkumar, your immense care and guidance have been my compass, always pointing me toward resilience and wisdom. To my Mumma, Tamil Selvi, your boundless love has been my greatest source of strength, grounding me through every phase of life.

To my sister, Manoranthini, and my brothers, Kaushick Kumar and Krishna, thank you for being my lifelong companions and sharing my joys, laughter, and growth. Your presence has made this journey truly beautiful.

To my husband, P. Ramesh, the foundation of my being and the essence of my soul your steadfast belief in me, your love, and your encouragement have illuminated every path, even in the darkest times. You are my forever partner in love and purpose.

To my children, Arun Vithuran and Advaitha, my heartbeats and my anchors you are my endless inspiration. Your love and joy fuel my determination to grow, thrive, and give the best of myself to the world.

I bow in remembrance to my late grandparents, whose blessings I carry in my heart, and to my parents and extended family of friends and relatives your affection, support, and kindness have been my pillars of strength.

Lastly, to everyone who has crossed my path, whether briefly or for a lifetime, thank you. Each interaction, lesson, and moment of love has added richness to the tapestry of my life. I am deeply grateful to all of you for shaping the person I am today.

PROLOGUE

Master Your Journey

Life is a journey where you are your constant companion from the moment you're born until your last breath. No matter the circumstances, the challenges, or the pain you've endured, the responsibility for your life lies solely with you. You hold the power to navigate through emotions, face hardships, and shape your destiny. Blaming others or external factors won't change the course of your life owning it will.

To thrive, you must prioritize yourself. Be your greatest ally, your fiercest protector, and your truest friend. Your self-approval matters more than the validation of others. If something doesn't feel right, don't do it because no external disapproval will ever sting as much as letting yourself down.

Prioritizing yourself isn't selfish; it's necessary. When you take care of your needs, nurture your dreams, and honour your boundaries, you can offer your best self to the world. So, commit to being kind to yourself, listening to your inner voice, and living authentically. Never forget you are your greatest asset. Treat yourself accordingly.

3D Formula for a Better Life Journey

Discretion model

Discretion is judging and thinking critically before accepting or acting upon information. It encourages independent analysis rather than blindly believing what you hear, read, or watch. This approach fosters informed decisions based on personal understanding and reasoning, ensuring authenticity and clarity in your beliefs and actions.

Disapproval secret

Disapproval often arises when others lack the knowledge or understanding you possess. When they try to dismiss or undermine your ideas, remember that their reaction reflects their limitations, not your value. Don't fear their disapproval or let it diminish your confidence. Trust in yourself and your insights; their doubts; their thoughts, their mindset, it's all their problem, not yours.

Decision Mantra:

If it's good for you, strengthens your family, and benefits society, it's the right path to take. By embracing choices that meet all three elements, you align with a life of purpose, harmony, and contribution a life where your joy connects seamlessly with the joy of others.

Life is full of choices, but the right ones often align with a deeper purpose. When making decisions, ask yourself three key questions:

1. Is it good for me?

Does it align with your values, growth, and overall well-being?

2. Does it strengthen my family?

Will this decision bring harmony, love, and support to those closest to you?

3. Does it benefit society?

Will it contribute positively to the world around you, leaving a mark of goodness?

If the answer to all three is a resounding "yes," you've found your path forward. This mantra simplifies complexity and keeps you anchored in purpose.

Butterfly Unfolded

Setting the Stage

Reflect on a metaphor that beautifully parallels our life's journey: the lifecycle of a butterfly. From an egg's humble beginnings to the butterfly's awe-inspiring flight, this transformation is a testament to resilience, growth, and the power of perseverance.

Let's start with the egg. This represents the inception of our dreams and aspirations. At this stage, our ideas are fragile, full of potential, but vulnerable to external forces. Just like not every egg hatches into a caterpillar, not all dreams take root. It requires the right environment, nurturing, and courage to move forward.

Then comes the larva, or the caterpillar stage a phase of relentless growth. This is when we immerse ourselves in learning, facing challenges head-on, and acquiring the resources needed for our future. However, growth isn't always linear; it's messy, uncomfortable, and often exhausting. But this stage teaches us the value of hard work and discipline.

Next is the pupal stage a time of stillness and transformation. This is the dark phase, where the caterpillar is enclosed in a chrysalis. From the outside, it appears nothing is happening, but inside, profound change is taking place. Similarly, in our lives, there are periods of struggle, isolation, and uncertainty. These moments test our resolve. They force us to confront our fears and ask ourselves: Do we truly wish to transform?

Many give up during this stage, unable to endure the pain or see the bigger picture. But for those who persist, who embrace the struggle, a miracle unfolds. The chrysalis cracks open, and a butterfly emerges resilient, vibrant, and free.

The butterfly symbolizes success, fulfilment, and self-realization. But its journey teaches us that success doesn't come without effort. Every phase, from egg to butterfly, is essential. And just as not every egg becomes a butterfly, not everyone reaches their full potential. The difference lies in the choices we make during the struggles.

So, I leave you with this thought: Are you ready to embrace the challenges, endure the darkness, and emerge as the butterfly you are meant to be?

Being like a butterfly in your life means embracing transformation and growth while staying patient and resilient through challenges. Here are some ways you can unfold your butterfly-like qualities in your life:

1. Start Small, Dream Big (Egg Stage)

Start with a clear goal or dream, even if it feels small. Every great achievement begins with a tiny idea or effort. Focus on planting the seeds of habits, relationships, and passions that you want to nurture over time.

2. Be Hungry to Grow (Caterpillar Stage)

Keep learning and growing. Take on challenges, build skills, and step outside your comfort zone. Like the caterpillar eats to prepare, fill yourself with knowledge and experiences. This is your "active" phase. Take care of your health, practice discipline, and work consistently toward your goals.

3. Embrace the Hard Times (Chrysalis Stage)

When you face setbacks or feel stuck, remember this is where deep transformation happens. Use this time to reflect, plan, and reimagine your path. Trust the process. Life will have moments of stillness or struggle. Instead of resisting them, see them as opportunities for inner growth, resilience, and self-discovery.

4. Break Free and Take Flight (Butterfly Stage)

Share your talents, ideas, and hard work with the world. Celebrate your accomplishments but stay humble your journey continues. Live fully and authentically. Appreciate the beauty of the present moment, share your joy with others, and use your growth to inspire and uplift those around you.

5. Trust the Cycle

Life, like a butterfly's journey, is cyclical. You'll go through multiple phases of growth, struggle, and transformation. Keep setting new goals and embracing change. After every success, prepare for the next stage of learning. Understand that setbacks don't mean failure they are part of your transformation. Stay open to change and keep evolving.

6. Spread Your Wings and Be Free

Butterflies don't hold back. They move gracefully, enjoying the world around them. Be bold in your ideas and actions. Take pride in what you've achieved but stay curious and explore new opportunities. Let go of self-doubt and comparisons. Be kind to yourself, embrace your unique journey, and live with purpose and joy.

Time to fly

Living like a butterfly means remembering that every phase has a purpose. Work hard, trust yourself during the tough times, and celebrate the beauty of transformation. When you approach life this way, you'll find that even the smallest steps can lead to a life that's as vibrant and free as the butterfly's flight.

I

The Analogy of Systems

In the modern age of technology, comparing the human body to a computer is both fascinating and insightful. The analogy reveals the intricate interplay between physical and mental health, emotional well-being, and spiritual wellness, all functioning as parts of a sophisticated system. Like a computer, the human system consists of hardware and software, with each component intricately affecting the other.

The Hardware: Physical and Mental Health

The hardware of a computer represents its tangible components — the processor, memory, and storage devices. Similarly, the human body's hardware encompasses physical and mental health. Just as a computer relies on its hardware to function smoothly, our bodies depend on their physical and mental capacities to operate effectively.

1. Physical Health: The body serves as the outer shell of our system, akin to the computer's casing and circuits. Proper nutrition, exercise, and sleep ensure that this hardware remains functional and resilient. Neglect, however, can lead to wear and tear, just as a poorly maintained computer can slow down or break.

2. Mental Health: The mind acts as an essential component of the hardware, processing thoughts and decisions. Like a computer's processor, the brain coordinates all functions, ensuring that data flows seamlessly. A well-maintained mind can solve problems efficiently, while stress or mental overload can cause system "lag."

The Software: Emotional and Spiritual Wellness

The software is what brings a computer to life, enabling it to perform various tasks. In the human system, emotional and spiritual wellness represent the intangible yet essential elements that define our quality of life.

1. Emotional Well-being: This is the operating system that runs daily tasks. Our emotions, shaped by experiences and thoughts, dictate our interactions and decisions. Positive emotions can optimize performance, while unresolved negativity acts as malware, disrupting the system.

2. Spiritual Wellness: Beyond emotions lies a deeper layer of software our sense of purpose and connection. Spiritual wellness provides the guiding framework, much like specialized software enhances a computer's capabilities. It ensures that the system remains aligned with its core values and functions meaningfully.

Input Data, Consciousness, and Memory

The human experience is driven by thoughts, which serve as input data. These thoughts enter our conscious mind, represented by the computer's RAM (Random Access Memory). The conscious mind processes this data in real-time, determining our immediate reactions and decisions. However, not all data remains in the RAM; much of it is stored in the subconscious mind, akin to the hard disk. This storage houses deep-seated beliefs, habits, and memories, influencing how the system functions over time.

The CPU: The Brain at the Helm

At the center of the system lies the CPU (Central Processing Unit), which is analogous to the human brain. The CPU manages the overall process, executing commands, interpreting data, and ensuring harmony between hardware and software. A well-functioning brain can lead the system to excel, while a compromised brain can result in inefficiency or errors.

Habits and the Compound Effect

Our daily emotions and habits shape the system's long-term performance. Positive habits, such as gratitude, mindfulness, and exercise, serve as regular updates and patches, enhancing software and hardware compatibility. Over time, these habits compound, leading to a harmonious and efficient system. Conversely, unchecked negative habits act as viruses, corrupting the software and causing wear on the hardware. Prolonged negativity can manifest as chronic illnesses, showing how deeply intertwined the two aspects are.

The Balance of Hardware and Software

For a computer to function optimally, its hardware and software must work in harmony. Similarly, human satisfaction and well-being emerge when physical health, mental clarity, emotional balance, and spiritual alignment coexist. A system in balance is resilient, adaptable, and capable of overcoming challenges, while an unbalanced system risks breakdowns and chronic dysfunction.

Inference

The comparison between a human body and a computer system offers profound insights into how we operate as individuals. By maintaining our hardware through physical and mental care, and nurturing our software with emotional and spiritual well-being, we can ensure that our system remains efficient and fulfilling. Ultimately, just as a well-maintained computer serves its purpose for years, a balanced human system can lead to a life of satisfaction and vitality.

To truly optimize the human system, it is essential to recognize the interconnectedness between all components. Ignoring one aspect, whether hardware or software, can lead to cascading failures. For instance, prolonged stress (a software issue) can manifest as physical ailments like hypertension or fatigue (hardware issues). Similarly, neglecting physical health through poor diet or lack of exercise can cloud emotional well-being and hinder spiritual growth.

Routine Maintenance: Updates and Troubleshooting

Just as a computer requires regular updates and maintenance, so too does the human body and mind. This upkeep involves intentional actions:

1. Physical Maintenance: Regular exercise, balanced nutrition, and sufficient rest are the foundation of a healthy system. These habits ensure that the hardware remains robust and capable of supporting the software's demands.

2. Mental and Emotional Updates: Practicing mindfulness, therapy, or journaling can help identify and resolve emotional "bugs." These activities provide clarity and ensure that outdated or harmful beliefs in the subconscious are replaced with constructive ones.

3. Spiritual Recalibration: Periodic reflection, meditation, or engaging in meaningful practices can realign our internal compass. This ensures that our software operates in harmony with our core values, offering long-term satisfaction.

4. Error Handling and Debugging: Life often introduces challenges that test our system. Developing resilience and adaptability is akin to installing an advanced antivirus program, allowing us to detect and neutralize threats before they cause lasting damage.

The Ripple Effect on the Environment

A well-functioning human system not only benefits the individual but also creates a positive ripple effect on their surroundings. A person with balanced hardware and software is more likely to contribute positively to relationships, work, and society. Their efficient system becomes a model for others, fostering a healthier collective environment.

Conversely, a system plagued by neglect or imbalance can project negativity, affecting both personal and professional interactions. This highlights the importance of self-awareness and proactive care, not just for personal growth but for the greater good.

Lessons from the Analogy

This comparison between the human body and a computer system reminds us of several key lessons:

Integration is Key: Both hardware and software are essential. Neglecting one compromises the other. We must prioritize both physical health and emotional-spiritual well-being to achieve balance.

Small Actions Compound: Just as routine updates and backups prevent a computer from crashing, small daily habits can have a profound long-term impact on our system's functionality.

Awareness and Adaptation: Staying attuned to system performance allows us to identify issues early and adjust. Being adaptable in the face of life's challenges ensures sustained functionality and satisfaction.

The Need for a Holistic Approach: Addressing one part of the system in isolation is insufficient. A truly optimized human system requires a holistic approach, blending physical care, emotional intelligence, and spiritual awareness.

Summary

By viewing the human body as a complex system of hardware and software, we gain a clearer understanding of the intricate balance needed for a fulfilling life. Our thoughts, habits, and daily actions shape this system, reflecting a compound effect over time. Whether the system thrives or deteriorates depends on our choices. Like a well-maintained computer, a balanced human system can lead to remarkable achievements, resilience, and satisfaction. The challenge lies in nurturing every component, ensuring that we remain not only functional but extraordinary.

ANUSHRI RAMESH

II
Why Balance is Key

Fitness is often misunderstood as merely having a physically fit appearance, such as showing off biceps or six-pack abs. However, this idealized version of fitness is short-lived; the human body can only sustain such a state temporarily. Many live in a fantasy world, imagining themselves with bodies like Shah Rukh Khan or Hrithik Roshan, yet they take no meaningful steps to achieve it, often gaining weight instead, sometimes resembling a sumo wrestler. For some, even crossing 100 kilograms is not seen as a significant issue.

In today's digital world, overwhelmed by conflicting information, people often dismiss their weight by justifying, "Age is just a number, and so is weight." When someone suggests adopting a healthier lifestyle through diet or exercise, it's often dismissed as body shaming or discrimination.

Breaking the Fitness Stigma

Fitness is not about merely looking good on the outside; it begins from within. While people focus intensely on physical appearance, they often neglect the connection between their mind and body. The world is now starting to talk more about mental health and seeking help when needed, yet we forget the importance of prevention and nurturing our overall well-being from scratch.

Fitness is not a one-size-fits-all concept; it encompasses many facets of life. It involves four major aspects: body, mind, soul, and spirit. True fitness is about achieving a balanced state of physical, mental, emotional, and spiritual health.

Survival of the fittest doesn't just apply to physical strength; it's about holistic adaptability. Fitness is the ability to adapt, endure, and thrive in all aspects of life—physically, mentally, emotionally, and spiritually. While physical fitness is often glorified, true fitness comes from balance across these dimensions.

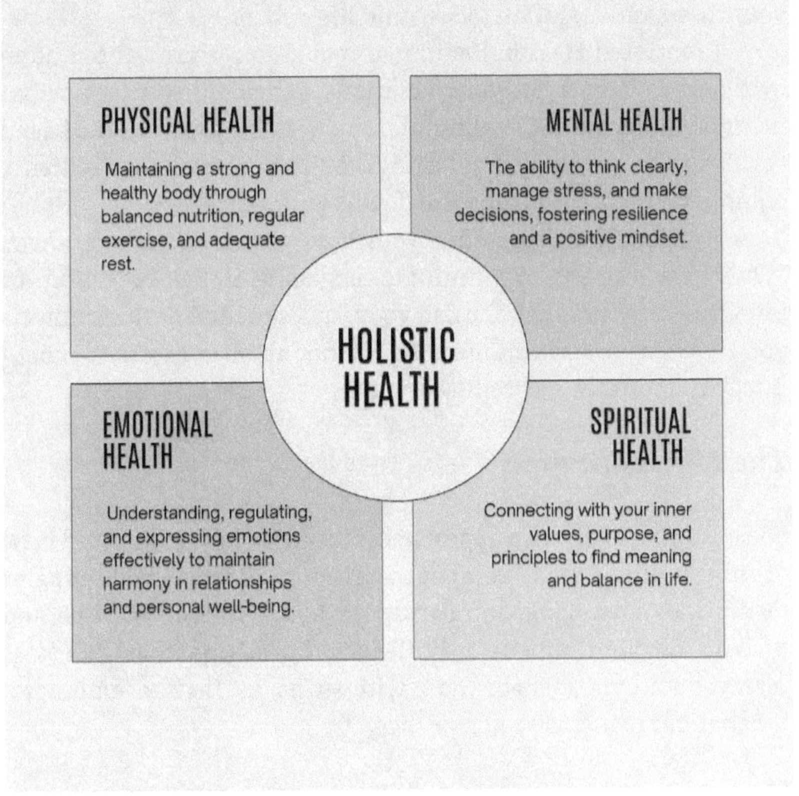

Image of Holistic Health

Practical Steps Toward Holistic Health

1. Physical Health: Start small. You don't need to spend hours at the gym or follow extreme diets. Focus on sustainable habits such as walking daily, eating balanced meals, and prioritizing sleep. Remember, what you put into your body has a direct impact on your energy, mood, and overall health.

2. Mental Health: Cultivate a positive mindset. Engage in activities that challenge your brain, like reading, solving puzzles, or learning new skills. Practice mindfulness and meditation to calm your mind and maintain focus amid life's chaos.

3. Emotional Health: Emotional regulation is crucial but often overlooked. Reflect on your emotions and identify triggers that disrupt your peace. Journaling, therapy, or talking to a trusted friend can help you process your feelings. Building emotional resilience equips you to face life's ups and downs with grace.

4. Spiritual Health: Define your core values and live by them. Whether it's practicing gratitude, engaging in self-reflection, or pursuing activities that nourish your soul, spiritual health connects you to a deeper sense of purpose. It's not about religion; it's about integrity, morality, and self-awareness.

The Fitness Stigma

Society's obsession with appearances often leads to a distorted view of fitness. Being fit is not about achieving a certain body type or fitting into unrealistic standards. It's about finding balance and thriving in your unique way. Reject the stigma that fitness is reserved for gym-goers or those with six-packs. Instead, embrace a broader, more inclusive perspective.

Your Fitness Journey

Embarking on a fitness journey can be overwhelming, but remember, it's not a race. Start where you are, and focus on progress, not perfection. Celebrate small victories and forgive yourself for setbacks. Fitness is not about comparison; it's about becoming the best version of yourself.

Survival of the Fittest: A Timeless Concept

Charles Darwin's theory of evolution emphasizes that survival is not guaranteed to the strongest or the smartest but to those who are most adaptable to change. This concept applies to every aspect of life, including fitness. It isn't just about physical survival in a harsh environment but thriving in the ever-changing circumstances of modern life.

In today's world, "fitness" extends beyond the biological realm. It encompasses mental resilience, emotional adaptability, and spiritual grounding. While Darwin's theory initially focused on species adapting to environmental challenges, it now serves as a metaphor for how individuals can cope with the complexities of contemporary living.

Adapting to Life's Challenges

Physical Adaptability: In prehistoric times, physical fitness was critical for survival escaping predators, finding food, and enduring harsh climates. Today, the challenges may have changed, but physical fitness remains essential. Sedentary lifestyles, unhealthy diets, and chronic stress have become modern predators. Adapting to these involves staying active, making conscious food choices, and prioritizing rest and recovery.

Mental Adaptability: Mental fitness is the cornerstone of thriving in a fast-paced, information-heavy world. The ability to adapt your mindset to shifting circumstances whether it's a career change, personal setback, or global crisis is key to surviving and thriving. Cultivating a growth mindset, where challenges are viewed as opportunities to learn, is an evolved form of mental adaptability.

Emotional Adaptability: Emotional intelligence—the ability to understand, regulate, and respond to your own emotions and those of others is a modern-day survival skill. Life is full of emotional turbulence, and those who can navigate their feelings while maintaining their well-being are better equipped to thrive in social and personal settings.

Spiritual Adaptability: Spiritual fitness fosters resilience by connecting us to something greater than ourselves. It encourages introspection, clarity of purpose, and the moral compass needed to navigate life's challenges. People who align their actions with their values and principles often find it easier to adapt to changes and maintain inner peace.

Modern-Day Survival

In the context of today's challenges technological advancements, global crises, and societal pressures survival of the fittest takes on new meanings:

1. Workplace Evolution: The modern work environment demands constant skill upgrades and adaptability. Those who can pivot, learn, and innovate in response to changes in technology and market demands are more likely to succeed.

2. Social Survival: With the rise of social media, maintaining authenticity while adapting to societal expectations is crucial. Emotional intelligence and empathy have become vital tools for navigating relationships in the digital age.

3. Health and Wellness: The fitness industry often promotes unrealistic body standards, but true survival lies in adopting a sustainable and balanced approach to health. Being "fit" means having the stamina to enjoy life, the mental clarity to solve problems, and the emotional strength to face adversity.

Fitness Through Adaptability

To truly embody the survival of the fittest theory, focus on building adaptability across all dimensions of life:

Be flexible: Embrace change as an opportunity rather than a threat.

Prioritize holistic health: Balance physical activity with mental and emotional well-being.

Stay curious: Continuously learn and grow, both intellectually and emotionally.

Cultivate resilience: View setbacks as stepping stones to greater achievements.

Fitness is no longer a measure of muscles or aesthetics; it is the art of adapting to an ever-changing world while maintaining balance and authenticity. As Darwin's theory suggests, survival isn't about being the strongest but about evolving to meet life's challenges head-on.

Hierarchy of need

The image represents Maslow's Hierarchy of Needs, a psychological framework that organizes human needs into five levels. These levels are depicted as a pyramid, with the most basic needs forming the foundation and more abstract needs building on top. Here's how each level connects:

1. Physiological Needs (Base of the Pyramid)

These are the most fundamental needs such as food, water, air, sleep, and shelter. Without meeting these, survival is impossible. For example, when someone is hungry or in physical pain, their primary focus is on alleviating that discomfort they can't think about anything else until these needs are met.

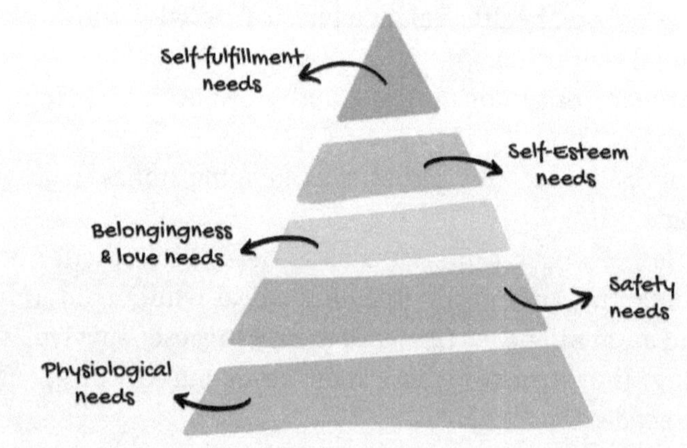

Maslow's Hierarchy of Needs

2. Safety Needs

Once physiological needs are satisfied, the focus shifts to safety and security. This includes physical safety (protection from harm), financial stability, health, and a secure environment. Without this sense of safety, the mind is preoccupied with avoiding threats, leaving no room for higher-level aspirations.

3. Belongingness and Love Needs

After ensuring safety, humans crave connection, love, and acceptance. This level includes friendships, intimate relationships, and social groups. Without emotional connections, people may feel isolated, which can impact mental and emotional health. However, these connections are only meaningful when the body feels safe and nourished.

4. Self-Esteem Needs

Once a person feels loved and accepted, they seek self-respect and recognition. This includes confidence, achievements, and feeling valued. People cannot focus on their self-worth if they're struggling with unmet emotional or safety needs.

5. Self-Fulfilment Needs (Top of the Pyramid)

At the peak lies self-actualization the desire to achieve one's full potential, pursue creativity, and find purpose. However, this is only attainable when all the foundational needs are met, allowing the mind to focus on growth rather than survival.

Key Insight:

When you're in pain be it physical, mental, or emotional—it becomes the dominant issue that blocks your ability to focus on anything else. For instance, physical pain overshadows emotional or intellectual concerns, just as unmet safety or belongingness needs to overshadow ambitions for self-esteem or fulfilment. This hierarchy reminds us to address the most pressing needs first, acknowledging that human growth is a step-by-step process.

Physical Health – The Hardware

III

1. The Body as the Foundation

The Foundation of Physical Health: A Holistic Approach

Physical health is built upon several key pillars: proper nutrition, quality sleep, a robust immune system, balanced hormones, and sustainable habits. To thrive physically, it's essential to understand how these elements work together and how to support them daily.

Nutrients: The Building Blocks of Health

Nutrients fuel our bodies, repair tissues, and support vital functions. They are broadly categorized into macronutrients (carbohydrates, proteins, and fats) and micronutrients (vitamins and minerals).

Proteins: These are essential for building muscles, repairing tissues, and creating enzymes and hormones. Sources include Animal-based: Eggs, chicken, fish, and dairy. Plant-based: Lentils, beans, tofu, tempeh, quinoa, and nuts.

Fiber: Crucial for digestive health, fibre regulates blood sugar, lowers cholesterol, and feeds gut bacteria. Sources include: Fruits like apples, oranges, pomegranates, papaya, melons, bananas, and berries. Vegetables include cauliflower, cucumber, okra, brinjal, broccoli, spinach, beetroot, and carrots—whole grains like millet, oats, brown rice, and whole wheat.

Fats: Healthy fats are vital for brain function, hormone production, and energy; opt for avocados, nuts, seeds, olive oil, and fatty fish like salmon.

Micronutrients: Vitamins (like Vitamin D, C, and B12) and minerals (such as calcium, magnesium, and zinc) support everything from immune function to bone health. A diverse diet ensures adequate intake.

The Role of Sleep in Physical Health

Sleep is often underestimated but is essential for recovery and overall well-being. During sleep, the body repairs tissues and muscles, balances hormones such as cortisol and melatonin, and strengthens the immune system by producing infection-fighting molecules.

Tips for Better Sleep:

Maintain a consistent sleep schedule. Avoid caffeine and screens 1-2 hours before bedtime. Create a relaxing bedtime routine, such as reading or meditation.

Immunity and Hormonal Balance

A strong immune system and balanced hormones are central to physical health.

Boosting Immunity:
Regular intake of antioxidants (found in fruits and vegetables) and probiotics (in fermented foods) strengthens immunity. Exercise

and stress management are also crucial.

Hormonal Balance:

Hormones regulate appetite, metabolism, mood, and sleep. Support hormonal health by eating healthy fats (to aid hormone production). Avoiding excessive sugar and processed foods. Staying hydrated.

Way of Eating: Mindful and Balanced

The way you eat is as important as what you eat. Adopting mindful eating practices ensures that the body absorbs nutrients effectively. Eat slowly and chew thoroughly. Maintain a balanced plate with proteins, carbohydrates, and fats. Include plenty of colourful vegetables and fruits. Opt for whole, minimally processed foods.

Importance of Fermented Foods

Fermented foods are rich in probiotics, which are beneficial bacteria that improve gut health and immunity. Regular consumption can enhance digestion, improve nutrient absorption, and reduce inflammation.

Examples of fermented foods include yogurt, kefir, buttermilk, kimchi, sauerkraut, and pickles. Fermented soy products like tempeh and miso.

Developing Healthy Food Habits

- Plan: Prepare meals in advance to avoid unhealthy choices.
- Stay Hydrated: Drink at least 8-10 glasses of water daily.
- Practice Portion Control: Overeating, even healthy foods, can strain the digestive system.
- Include Variety: Rotate your meals to cover a wide range of nutrients.

- Limit Sugar and Salt: Excess consumption can lead to chronic diseases.

A Holistic View of Physical Health

Optimal physical health is a synergy of good nutrition, quality sleep, a balanced lifestyle, and emotional well-being. It's not about perfection but consistency in habits. Small, sustainable changes, such as adding a serving of vegetables to every meal or taking a 10-minute walk after eating, can make a significant difference over time. By focusing on these foundational principles, you create a resilient body and mind capable of withstanding stress and disease, ensuring long-term health and vitality.

Exercise and Physical Activity: A Crucial Component of Physical Health

While proper nutrition and sleep are vital, physical activity plays an indispensable role in maintaining and improving physical health. Regular exercise strengthens the heart, muscles, and bones, improves mental clarity, and boosts mood. Physical activity also helps balance hormones, regulate blood sugar levels, and support a healthy immune system.

Cardiovascular Exercise: Activities like walking, jogging, swimming, and cycling help maintain heart health, improve circulation, and enhance lung function.

Strength Training: Resistance exercises, such as weightlifting or bodyweight exercises (like squats, push-ups, and lunges), help build muscle mass, boost metabolism, and strengthen bones.

Flexibility and Mobility: Practices like yoga, pilates, and stretching help improve flexibility, reduce muscle tension, and prevent injury.

The general recommendation is to aim for at least 30 minutes of moderate-intensity exercise most days of the week, combining different forms of physical activity for overall health.

Mental and Emotional Health: Its Impact on Physical Well-being

The mind and body are deeply interconnected, and emotional well-being plays a crucial role in physical health. Chronic stress, anxiety, and depression can lead to hormonal imbalances (such as increased cortisol), weakened immunity, and even disruptions in sleep patterns. On the other hand, positive mental health fosters a healthy physical body.

Stress Management: Engage in mindfulness practices like meditation, deep breathing, and journaling to manage stress effectively.

Social Connections: Strong, supportive relationships are key to emotional well-being. Socializing with friends and family promotes happiness, reducing the negative impact of stress on the body.

Mental Rest: Just as your body needs physical rest, your mind requires downtime. Practice relaxation techniques, limit exposure to negative media, and ensure you have leisure activities that nurture your emotional health.

The Importance of Consistency in Lifestyle

A healthy lifestyle is not about drastic changes but small, consistent efforts. For example, opting for home-cooked meals over take-out, getting an extra 15 minutes of sleep each night, or replacing sugary snacks with fruits can have a significant impact over time. Consistency in daily habits leads to lasting results in physical health.

Tracking Progress: Whether it's through journaling, tracking meals, or logging workouts, keeping track of your health journey can help you stay motivated and focused.

Staying Flexible: Life can be unpredictable, and there will be times when you're unable to stick to your routine. It's important to be adaptable, not overly critical of yourself, and to get back on track with your next meal or activity.

The Role of Hydration in Physical Health

Water is often overlooked but is a crucial aspect of physical health. Every cell in the body relies on water for optimal function. Hydration supports digestion, helps flush toxins from the body, regulates body temperature, and even affects mental clarity and mood.

How Much Water Should You Drink?

The general recommendation is to drink at least 8 glasses (about 2 litres) of water daily, but individual needs may vary depending on activity level, age, and environmental factors.

Hydration and Nutrition: Consuming hydrating foods like cucumbers, watermelon, and oranges can supplement your daily fluid intake. Avoid sugary drinks and excessive caffeine, which can lead to dehydration.

The Impact of Environmental Factors on Physical Health

In addition to nutrition, sleep, exercise, and mental health, external factors like pollution, exposure to toxins, and even your home or work environment can influence your physical well-being.

Air Quality: Pollution and poor air quality can have a detrimental effect on lung health and contribute to conditions such as asthma or cardiovascular disease. Ensuring good air circulation and using air purifiers can help mitigate this impact.

Toxins: Reducing exposure to chemicals in cleaning products, cosmetics, and plastic containers can protect your overall health. Opting for natural products whenever possible can decrease the toxic load on the body.

Natural Light: Sunlight is essential to produce Vitamin D, which is crucial for bone health, immune function, and mood regulation. Aim to get at least 15-30 minutes of sun exposure each day.

Integrating These Principles into Your Life

Integrating the principles of proper nutrition, sleep, exercise, hydration, stress management, and environmental health doesn't require perfection. Focus on progress, not perfection. Some simple ways to start integrating these habits into your life include:

Meal Prep: Plan your meals for the week to ensure you have balanced, nutritious options readily available.

Exercise Routine: Start with small, manageable goals and gradually increase intensity or duration as you get more comfortable.

Sleep Hygiene: Create a calming pre-sleep routine (like reading or meditating) and stick to a consistent sleep schedule.

Mindful Practices: Incorporate stress-relieving activities into your daily routine, such as deep breathing exercises or journaling.

Summary

Physical health is a dynamic and interconnected system that requires attention to multiple aspects of life. Proper nutrition, regular exercise, quality sleep, effective stress management, and hydration form the foundation of well-being. By fostering consistent healthy habits and remaining adaptable to life's changes, you create a resilient body and mind capable of thriving in all aspects of life. Remember, physical health isn't a destination but a continuous journey. Every small, consistent step you take toward better habits will ultimately lead to long-lasting health benefits.

IV

2. Breaking Weight Myths

I am a proud mother of two wonderful children: an exuberant son and a delightful daughter. Embarking on the journey of motherhood has been a life-altering experience, one that has brought profound lessons, formidable challenges, and moments of indescribable joy.

While my first pregnancy was relatively smooth, it concluded with an unanticipated cesarean delivery. In contrast, my second pregnancy was a journey of resilience and perseverance, marked by emotional turbulence and medical challenges. From managing respiratory issues in the first trimester to enduring febrile episodes in the second, and eventually addressing low amniotic fluid levels in the final weeks, each stage tested my physical and emotional strength.

However, all the trials paled in comparison to the overwhelming joy of welcoming my baby girl into the world. This journey has been transformative, not only deepening my understanding of motherhood but also reshaping my outlook on life itself. It has reinforced my unwavering belief in the power of maternal love, resilience, and determination.

My Postpartum Weight Loss Journey: A Story of Resilience and Transformation

The journey to losing 20 kilograms after my second pregnancy wasn't just about shedding weight it was a profound transformation of my mind, body, and spirit. My second pregnancy was fraught with health challenges, emotional struggles, and self-doubt, but it also became a testament to my resilience.

The Struggles of My Second Pregnancy

Unlike my first pregnancy, my second was marked by severe health issues. Persistent digestive problems, including vomiting and loose stools, left me physically weak. Wheezing further exacerbated my discomfort, and my diet became severely restricted. I couldn't tolerate fruits or vegetables, which made my nutrition suffer.

Adding to these physical challenges was the emotional turmoil. Initially, my husband and I had agreed not to have a second child. However, when faced with the decision, I couldn't bring myself to abort. This internal conflict weighed heavily on me, causing stress that worsened my health. Yet, amidst all the challenges, I decided to fight for myself, for my unborn baby, and for a brighter future. The day my daughter was born wasn't just her birthday; it was my rebirth.

Reclaiming My Health

Five months postpartum, I resolved to take control of my health. My daughter became my greatest motivation, reminding me every day of my strength. I embarked on a journey of physical and mental renewal, incorporating exercise, yoga, and meditation into my daily routine.

I started small, focusing on consistency rather than intensity. Gradually, my body adapted, and I found joy in moving again. Each workout wasn't just about burning calories it was a celebration of what my body could achieve.

Revamping My Relationship with Food

Food was another critical aspect of my transformation. I stopped obsessing over measurements or restrictive diets and instead focused on making my meals simple, healthy, and satisfying.

Balanced Platter: I made a conscious effort to include fibre, fermented foods, and at least one fruit daily for myself and my children.

Mindful Fasting: I embraced overnight fasting, typically for 12 hours, and started my mornings with water or, occasionally, apple cider vinegar to stabilize my glucose levels.

Flexible Eating: Some days, I eat two meals; other days, three depending on my body's needs and activity levels. I indulged in desserts guilt-free, prioritizing moderation over deprivation.

Cooking became a source of happiness and creativity for me. I incorporated nuts and seeds into curries, fibre into idly and dosa batters, and millets into fermented dishes. My approach was not to diet but to nourish my body, making healthy eating a sustainable lifestyle.

Listening to My Body

One of the most important lessons I learned was to trust my body's signals. On days when I wasn't hungry, I chose to fast. On days when I felt ravenous, I ate heartily. This intuitive approach allowed me to honour my body's needs without feeling pressured or guilty.

Even during premenstrual periods, when my cravings for sweets peaked, I allowed myself to enjoy dark chocolate my favourite treat. This balance ensured that I never felt deprived or frustrated.

A Year of Transformation

Over the course of a year, I experienced a remarkable transformation not just in weight, but in my overall happiness and well-being. I didn't view this journey as a struggle but as a path to reclaiming myself.

I became more aware of the nutrients in my food and adapted easily to new recipes and eating habits. My focus wasn't on losing weight but on building a healthier, stronger version of myself. This mindset shift made the journey less daunting and more fulfiling.

Reflections

Today, I look back on my postpartum journey with immense gratitude. The struggles of my second pregnancy taught me resilience, and my weight loss journey reaffirmed the power of self-love and determination.

Losing 20 kilograms wasn't just about numbers on a scale it was about finding balance, embracing my body, and prioritizing my well-being. My daughter, my greatest motivation, reminds me every day of the strength within me.

This journey has been a testament to the fact that, with the right mindset and a bit of patience, transformation is possible not just in appearance but in the quality of life.

Today, I feel more energetic, confident, and aligned with my goals. What started as a journey to lose weight became a deeper exploration of how food, movement, and mindfulness could transform not just my body but my outlook on life.

I've learned that self-care isn't selfish; it's essential. As a mother, I often put my children's needs first, but this journey taught me that taking care of myself allows me to show up better for them. I no longer feel guilty about setting aside time for exercise or preparing meals that prioritize my health.

Lessons Learned

1. Mindset is Everything

The biggest shift for me was moving away from seeing weight loss as a punishment or chore. Instead, I approached it as a celebration of my body's ability to heal and thrive. This positive mindset helped me stay consistent without feeling overwhelmed.

2. Small Steps Lead to Big Changes

I didn't overhaul my lifestyle overnight. Starting with small, manageable steps like overnight fasting or adding more fibre to meals helped me build sustainable habits. Over time, these small changes added up to a complete transformation.

3. Listen to Your Body

No two days are the same, and I've learned to be in tune with my body's needs. Whether it's taking a rest day, indulging in a craving, or pushing myself a little harder at the gym, I trust my instincts.

4. Consistency Over Perfection

I realized that perfection isn't the goal progress is. There were days when I skipped workouts or indulged in less healthy foods, but I didn't let that derail my progress. I returned to my routine the next day with renewed focus.

5. Health Overweight

While losing 20 kilograms was an achievement, what mattered most was how I felt. I was stronger, more energetic, and mentally at peace. These were the true markers of success for me.

Moving Forward

My weight loss journey has become a lifestyle. I no longer see healthy eating or exercise as temporary efforts but as integral parts of who I am. I've also become more mindful of teaching my children the importance of balanced eating and self-care.

Through this experience, I've learned to celebrate my body for all that it has endured and achieved. It carried life, endured hardships, and emerged stronger. I am proud of the person I've become not just for losing weight, but for rediscovering my strength, resilience, and self-worth.

This journey wasn't just about losing 20 kilograms. It was about gaining a new perspective on life, embracing the challenges, and coming out stronger. If there's one thing, I hope others take from my story, it's that transformation is possible for anyone. With patience, determination, and self-love, you can achieve not just your physical goals but a renewed sense of joy and purpose. For me, this isn't the end of the journey it's just the beginning of a healthier, more vibrant chapter of my life.

Understanding Glucose Spikes and How I Manage My Blood Sugar

Glucose spikes refer to the rapid increase in blood sugar levels that occur after eating foods that are high in carbohydrates or sugar. These spikes can be harmful to health, particularly for individuals with insulin resistance or those at risk of developing diabetes. However, managing glucose spikes through mindful food choices has been a key part of my journey to reclaim my health, especially after my postpartum experience. Here's how I manage my blood sugar levels and maintain overall well-being through simple yet effective food habits.

Managing Glucose Spikes with Thoughtful Food Choices

One of the first steps I took in managing my glucose levels was becoming more mindful of the foods I ate and the order in which I consumed them. Here's how I've structured my meals:

1. The Order of My Meals: Veggies, Protein, Carbs

I prioritize eating vegetables and protein before any carbohydrates in my meals. This order helps slow down the absorption of sugar from carbs into the bloodstream, which helps prevent a sudden spike in glucose levels. By starting with fibre-rich veggies and protein, I stabilize my blood sugar and avoid the crashes that often follow high-carb meals.

2. Apple Cider Vinegar Before Carbs

One of the key habits I've incorporated into my routine is drinking a small amount of apple cider vinegar before consuming carbs. Apple cider vinegar has been shown to improve insulin sensitivity and help lower blood sugar levels after meals. It helps delay the absorption of sugar into the bloodstream, thus reducing the glucose spike. I typically dilute a tablespoon of apple cider vinegar in a glass of water in the morning or before eating a carb-heavy meal. This simple habit has had a positive impact on my digestion, energy levels, and overall blood sugar control.

3. Choosing Whole Fruits Over Fruit Juices

While fruit juices are often marketed as healthy, they can lead to rapid glucose spikes due to their high sugar content and lack of fibre. I make it a point to choose whole fruits instead of fruit juices. Whole fruits contain fibre, which helps slow down the release of sugar into the bloodstream, keeping blood sugar levels more stable.

Fruits like apples, berries, and citrus are my go-to options, as they offer nutrients and antioxidants while keeping my blood sugar in check.

4. Guilt-Free Sugar at the End of My Meal

I've learned to indulge in sweets in a more balanced way. Instead of eating sugary snacks or desserts between meals, I choose to enjoy a small serving of guilt-free sugar at the end of my meal. This helps reduce the immediate impact of glucose spikes because the meal is already digested, and the sugar is absorbed more slowly. I indulge in dark chocolate or other low-sugar desserts without feeling guilty, knowing I'm being mindful of my blood sugar.

The Benefits of My Approach

Adopting this thoughtful approach to eating has made a significant difference in how my body feels. Not only have I been able to manage my weight and improve my digestion, but my energy levels have stabilized. I no longer crave sugary snacks or feel the urge to nibble between meals. By focusing on whole, nutrient-dense foods and giving my body the right balance of macronutrients, I've found that I can enjoy food without guilt, while also maintaining stable blood sugar levels.

Conclusion: A Loving Approach to Food

The key takeaway from my experience is that the way we approach food matters not just for managing glucose spikes but for overall health. By incorporating simple habits like eating in a specific order, using apple cider vinegar, choosing fruits over fruit juices, and indulging in sugar mindfully, I've been able to keep my system happy and balanced. The process has been one of loving nourishment, rather than restriction or guilt.

For anyone struggling with blood sugar levels, I highly recommend taking a closer look at how food is consumed rather than just focusing on what is being eaten. Small adjustments, like the ones I've made, can have a big impact on long-term health and happiness.

V

3. Daily Rituals for Longevity

Daily Habits for a Long, Healthy Life

1. Start Your Day with Positivity

Begin each morning with a smile, regardless of the challenges you face. The first thing you do in the morning sets the tone for your entire day. Avoid diving into social media or WhatsApp chats first thing, as it leads to procrastination and scattered focus. Instead, engage in mindful activities like walking with the first ray of the sun, journaling, deep breathing, or setting intentions for the day.

2. Prioritize Healthy Morning Nutrition

Your first meal can shape your energy levels throughout the day. Avoid sugary breakfasts like sweetened coffee, fruit juices, or pastries, as they can cause insulin spikes and subsequent energy crashes. Instead, start with protein or fibre (e.g., eggs, nuts, or seeds).

Follow with complex carbohydrates (e.g., whole grains or vegetables). It's okay to indulge in sweet tooth occasionally but aim for consistency most days.

3. Move Your Body

Incorporate movement into your morning routine, even if it's just 5–10 minutes of stretching, yoga, or light cardio. If mornings are busy, find creative ways to stay active, like taking the stairs or a short walk during the day. Remember, if you don't prioritize exercise now, it will become harder during busier or more stressful times.

4. Manage Caffeine and Meal Timings

Avoid caffeine after 4 PM to ensure restful sleep. Eat dinner early and aim for a lighter meal in the evening. It will help you to lose weight faster than any fancy diet routine. Stick to a consistent bedtime to maintain your circadian rhythm.

5. Track Your Sleep

Adequate sleep is crucial for physical and mental well-being. Avoid late-night habits, such as eating at midnight or staying up unnecessarily, as they disrupt hormonal balance and the body's natural repair processes. Women are more sensitive to these disruptions, which can manifest as irregular periods or mood swings.

6. Mindful Nutrition

Incorporate a variety of vegetables, fruits, pulses, and cereals into your diet. Balance animal proteins with plant-based options. Reserve a couple of days a week for nonvegetarian meals and stick to vegetarian rest of the days to diversify your nutrient intake and improve gut health. Avoid overeating oily, junk, or spicy foods, and instead focus on wholesome, home-cooked meals.

7. Hydration and Moderation

Stay hydrated throughout the day with plenty of water. Practice portion control and aim for a balanced, minimally processed diet.

8. Manage Stress and Responsibilities

Avoid taking on too many responsibilities at once. Delegate tasks, especially childcare, if you're a parent. Seek support when needed and create time for self-care.

9. Monitor Your Health

Women should track their menstrual cycles and mood changes to understand hormonal patterns. If you notice specific cravings (e.g., for spicy or oily foods), address them by increasing your intake of fresh fruits, vegetables, and fibre.

10. Avoid Harmful Habits

Midnight snacking, especially if it becomes habitual, can lead to metabolic issues, including an increased risk of cellular damage and long-term illnesses like cancer. Occasional indulgences are fine, but they should not become the norm.

11. Enhance Your Gut Health

A healthy gut is the cornerstone of overall well-being. Include fermented foods like yogurt, kefir, or homemade pickles in your diet to promote good bacteria. Rotating your grains, pulses, and vegetables can also improve digestion and nutrient absorption.

12. Stay Active Throughout the Day

If you have a sedentary job or lifestyle, take frequent breaks to stand, stretch, or walk. Engage in moderate physical activities like gardening, playing with children, or short exercise sessions. Cardio exercises, such as brisk walking, cycling, or dancing, are excellent for heart health.

13. Plan Your Meals Thoughtfully

Avoid skipping meals or overeating at irregular times. Stick to scheduled mealtimes as much as possible. Reduce eating out and prepare meals at home with fresh ingredients.

14. Avoid Processed and Packaged Foods

Processed foods, high in sugar, salt, and unhealthy fats, can lead to weight gain, inflammation, and chronic diseases. Replace snacks like chips or cookies with nuts, seeds, or fresh fruit.

15. Mindful Eating

Eat slowly and chew your food well to aid digestion. Avoid distractions like TV or scrolling on your phone while eating. Tune into your body's hunger and fullness signals.

16. Stay in Sync with Nature

Aligning your daily routine with natural rhythms helps maintain hormonal balance. Wake up early to enjoy sunlight, which regulates your sleep-wake cycle. Spend time outdoors to improve mood and reduce stress.

17. Practice Emotional Resilience

Don't let stress or setbacks take over your life. Getting up early 30 minutes before your routine brings an enormous change in your emotions you can do your work more peacefully than rushing to the office. Learn to adapt and stay positive. Practice gratitude daily, perhaps by journaling about things you are thankful for.

18. Build Supportive Relationships

Foster strong, loving relationships with family and friends. Share responsibilities and communicate openly to reduce stress.

19. Periodic Detox and Fasting

Occasionally giving your body, a break from continuous eating, such as through intermittent fasting, can improve metabolism and cellular repair. However, ensure you are well-nourished and consult a professional before starting any fasting regimen. Women can fast in the first week of their period helps to regulate bloating and digestive issues of periods as well and we can easily manage stress during this period.

20. Regular Health Checkups

Schedule regular medical checkups to monitor your overall health. Early detection of potential issues can make a significant difference in long-term health outcomes.

21. Limit Screen Time.

Prolonged exposure to screens, especially before bed, disrupts sleep and strains your eyes. Establish a digital curfew an hour before bedtime to wind down effectively.

22. Celebrate Small Wins

Acknowledge and reward yourself for the healthy habits you've maintained. It keeps you motivated and reinforces positive behaviour.

23. Prioritize Mental Health

Mental and emotional health are as important as physical health. Practice mindfulness or meditation to calm your mind. Seek therapy or talk to someone you trust if you feel overwhelmed.

24. Be Flexible Yet Committed

Life is unpredictable, and rigid routines can sometimes feel overwhelming. Give yourself grace on tough days. Skipping a workout or indulging in comfort food occasionally won't ruin your progress. The key is to return to your healthy habits consistently.

By integrating these habits into your lifestyle, you can improve not only your longevity but also the quality of your life. Consistency, mindfulness, and balance are the cornerstones of sustained well-being.

VI
Tools to Include

Health and Wellness Questionnaire

Physical Health

1. How would you rate your overall physical health on a scale of 1 to 10?

2. How often do you engage in physical activity (e.g., walking, exercise, sports)?

3. Do you experience any chronic pain or discomfort? If yes, where and how often?

4. How many hours of sleep do you get on average per night?

5. Do you feel well-rested when you wake up?

6. How often do you consume fruits and vegetables daily?

7. Do you eat home-cooked meals or rely on processed or restaurant food?

8. Are you currently maintaining a healthy weight for your age and height?

9. How often do you consume sugary drinks, alcohol, or caffeine?

10. Do you have regular checkups with a doctor or dentist?

Mental and Emotional Health

11. How would you rate your stress levels on a scale of 1 to 10?

12. How do you manage (e.g., meditation, journaling, therapy)?

13. Do you experience feelings of anxiety, sadness, or overwhelm frequently?

14. How often do you take time for self-care or hobbies?

15. Do you have a strong support system of friends or family to talk to?

16. Do you feel satisfied with your work-life balance?

17. Are there unresolved issues in your personal or professional life affecting your mental health?

Diet and Nutrition

18. How many meals do you eat daily, and are they balanced in nutrients?

19. Do you track your water intake? How much water do you drink daily?

20. Are you aware of any food intolerances or allergies?

21. Do you frequently experience bloating, indigestion, or other digestive issues?

22. How often do you eat junk or processed foods?

23. Do you include enough protein, fibre, and healthy fats in your diet?

Sleep Patterns

24. What time do you usually go to bed and wake up?

25. Do you use screens (phone, TV, etc.) before bed?

26. Do you wake up during the night, and if so, why?

27. How often do you feel tired or drowsy during the day?

28. Do you have a consistent bedtime routine?

Lifestyle and Habits

29. How much time do you spend sitting daily (e.g., at work, commuting)?

30. Do you smoke or use tobacco products?

31. How often do you consume alcohol, and in what quantity?

32. Do you prioritize movement, like walking, stretching, or taking the stairs, during the day?

33. How much time do you spend outdoors in natural light?

34. How often do you take breaks from work or other responsibilities?

Women's Health (if applicable)

35. Are your menstrual cycles regular, and do you experience any severe symptoms?

36. Do you track your menstrual cycle or hormonal changes?

37. Have you experienced any recent changes in your reproductive health?

38. Are you currently pregnant, breastfeeding, or planning to conceive?

Preventive Health

39. Have you had any recent medical checkups, such as blood tests or screenings?

40. Are you up to date with vaccinations and preventive measures?

41. Do you monitor your blood pressure, cholesterol, or blood sugar levels regularly?

42. Do you experience recurring headaches, fatigue, or other symptoms that could indicate an underlying issue?

General Well-being

43. Do you feel energized and motivated most days?

44. Are you satisfied with your current level of fitness and strength?

45. How do you typically spend your leisure time?

46. Are there any habits you'd like to change or improve?

47. Do you feel you understand your health needs and goals well?

48. Do you engage in regular activities that bring you joy or relaxation?

Long-term Goals and Vision

49. What are your primary health and wellness goals for this year?

50. Are you currently taking any steps to improve your health, and if so, what are they?

These questions can serve as a self-assessment or a discussion guide with a healthcare professional to better understand your health and wellness.

Mental Health – The Software

VII

4. Thought Streams: How the Mind Shapes Reality

The mind can be thought of as a powerful software, continuously processing inputs from your surroundings what you see, hear, feel, and consume. These inputs become the raw material for your thoughts, shaping your emotions, beliefs, and actions. While you may not have full control over the inputs that come your way, you can guide the stream of your thoughts in a constructive direction.

Conscious Mind: The Driver of Intentions

Your conscious mind is like the analytical control centre. It could think critically, analyse situations, and decide what to focus on. This is where you exercise discretion. It's crucial to develop the habit of questioning and evaluating everything you hear whether it comes from friends, family, books, or even your closest loved ones. Blindly accepting others' opinions, no matter how well-intentioned, can lead you astray.

Instead, rely on your own reasoning to conclude. This process of independent analysis is the hallmark of intelligence. However, being intelligent often attracts criticism, envy, and attempts to diminish your self-worth. Remember, such negativity stems from others' thoughts and insecurities, not your truth.

Subconscious Mind: The Seat of Beliefs

"Your subconscious mind operates as the repository of emotions, beliefs, values, and routines. It accepts what you deeply believe about yourself, whether positive or negative. For instance, if you consistently believe you are capable, smart, and lovable, your subconscious will align your behaviour and outcomes with these beliefs. This is the foundation of teachings in books like The Power of Your Subconscious Mind."

Changing ingrained values or routines requires deep and unwavering faith in your ability to transform. Without self-belief, no external force can install confidence or make meaningful changes for you. You are the gatekeeper of your own growth.

Resilience Through Emotional Mastery

Life's challenges often test your mental and emotional strength. When you face hardships, brokenness, or betrayal, it's easy to let anger, frustration, or despair take over. However, resilience is forged in such moments. Cultivating control over your emotions, especially in the face of adversity is a testament to the power of the mind.

Those who grow up in overly sheltered environments may struggle to develop this resilience. But through repeated experiences of overcoming, you build a powerful inner strength that allows you to rise again and again, no matter how many times you fall.

Discretion and Faith: Your Ultimate Tools

Ultimately, developing discretion and faith is the key to mastering your mind. Discretion enables you to sift through external influences and focus on what truly matters. Faith empowers you to believe in your ability to shape your reality, regardless of others' opinions or circumstances.

Trust yourself, know your worth, and remain steadfast in believing you can direct your mind toward greatness. This inner mastery is the essence of living a fulfilled and empowered life.

Decision Mantra: Choosing What's Right Over What's Easy

Life is full of decisions, and the paths you choose often define your destiny. When making decisions in life, follow this rule: Easy choices often lead to short-term comfort but may not benefit you in the long run. Hard choices can be challenging but often lead to growth and success.

Keep choosing what is truly good for you, even when it's difficult because that's where real progress lies. The key is to consistently do what aligns with your well-being and long-term growth, even if it feels heavy at the moment.

1. Short-Term Pain, Long-Term Gain

Choosing the hard but right thing often requires discipline, sacrifice, and perseverance. Sticking to a healthy routine may feel tough initially, but it leads to a stronger body and mind. Standing by your values in difficult situations might isolate you temporarily, but it strengthens your integrity and self-respect. On the other hand, easy options like procrastination, indulgence, or avoiding confrontation may provide comfort now but often lead to regret later.

2. Consistency Over Convenience

The secret to sustained success is doing what is good for you repeatedly, regardless of how it feels. Decisions like investing time in learning and personal growth. Nurturing meaningful relationships instead of shallow connections. Saying no to toxic influences, even if it feels uncomfortable. All these require effort, but they yield a life of fulfilment and purpose.

3. Emotional Detachment in Decision-Making

Sometimes, emotions cloud judgment. Fear of failure, guilt, or the desire to please others might push you toward easier, less beneficial choices. Develop the habit of pausing before deciding. Ask yourself:

Does this align with my values?

Is this choice building my future or sabotaging it?

Will I be proud of this decision later?

Detach from immediate gratification and focus on the bigger picture.

4. The Power of Doing the Right Thing

When you consistently choose what is good for you:

- Self-Trust Grows: You'll begin to trust your ability to make sound decisions.
- Resilience Strengthens: Hard things become easier as you build the mental muscle to handle challenges.
- Life Gains Meaning: Each choice adds to a life crafted intentionally rather than one dictated by convenience or fear.

5. Faith in the Journey

Making hard decisions doesn't mean life will immediately transform into perfection. It takes time for good habits and choices to compound. Have faith in the journey, knowing that each step toward what's good for you, no matter how small, brings you closer to the life you envision. By consistently choosing what nurtures your growth, you create a life rooted in authenticity, strength, and purpose.

Impact of Parenting and Circumstances

Parenting and early life circumstances profoundly shape a child's emotional, cognitive, and social development. A child's experiences during formative years influence their self-esteem, relationships, resilience, and overall mental health. When positive, these experiences lay the foundation for emotional stability and confidence. However, when negative or traumatic, they can have lasting effects into adulthood, often in ways the individual may not fully recognize.

1. Secure Attachment: Loving and supportive parenting fosters secure attachment, helping children feel safe and valued. Such individuals often grow into emotionally healthy adults who trust others and handle stress effectively.

2. Neglect or Over-criticism: Parents who are neglectful, overly critical, or emotionally unavailable may inadvertently damage a child's sense of self-worth, leading to anxiety, insecurity, or perfectionism in adulthood.

3. Trauma and Adversity: Adverse childhood experiences (ACEs) like abuse, neglect, or family dysfunction can disrupt brain development, leading to emotional dysregulation, hypervigilance, or avoidance behaviours later in life.

Impact of Childhood Trauma on Adulthood

Childhood trauma, if unresolved, can manifest as:

- Emotional Dysregulation: Difficulty managing emotions, leading to mood swings, anger, or numbness.
- Trust Issues: Difficulty forming or maintaining healthy relationships due to fear of vulnerability.
- Physical Symptoms: Chronic stress from unresolved trauma may lead to health issues such as fatigue, autoimmune disorders, or chronic pain.
- Mental Health Issues: Anxiety, depression, PTSD, or self-sabotaging behaviours can stem from unprocessed trauma.

Why Some Heal and Others Don't

1. Awareness and Recognition:

Some individuals recognize their trauma and seek help through therapy, self-reflection, or support groups. This awareness allows them to address the root causes of their pain. Others, however, may lack awareness or dismiss their trauma, using distractions like work, substance abuse, or toxic relationships to avoid confronting their feelings.

2. Support System:

A strong, empathetic support system can encourage healing, while a lack of support can perpetuate feelings of isolation and despair.

3. Personal Resilience and Resources:

Access to therapy, education, or coping strategies often determines whether someone can process and resolve their trauma.

Mental Health and Behavioural Impact

When trauma goes unaddressed, it can lead to behavioural changes, irritability, impulsivity, or withdrawal from loved ones. Cognitive Distortions by persistent negative thoughts about oneself or others, leading to low self-esteem or distrust. Mental health disorders lead to conditions like borderline personality disorder, chronic anxiety, or depression.

Healing from Childhood Trauma

1. Therapeutic Intervention:

Modalities like Cognitive Behavioural Therapy (CBT), Eye Movement Desensitization and Reprocessing (EMDR), or trauma-focused therapy can help individuals process and reframe their experiences.

2. Mindfulness and Self-awareness:

Practices like meditation, journaling, or mindfulness help individuals reconnect with their emotions and reduce reactivity to triggers.

3. Building Healthy Relationships:

Forming connections with empathetic and supportive individuals can provide the trust and validation needed to heal.

4. Addressing Negative Coping Mechanisms:

Identifying and replacing harmful behaviours with healthier alternatives is crucial to long-term recovery.

Unresolved childhood trauma creates cycles of pain that can affect an individual's life in profound ways. Recognizing and addressing this trauma is essential for breaking free from its grip. While healing is not linear, with the right resources, support, and determination, individuals can transform their pain into strength and regain control of their mental health and lives.

VIII

5. Insight and decluttering mind

Understanding Mental Health: The Uniqueness of Every Mind

Mental health, like physical health, is a tapestry woven from myriad threads of genetics, upbringing, environment, and personal experiences. Just as no two individuals share the same fingerprints, no two minds are wired alike. Each person's mental landscape is a dynamic interplay of biological predispositions, environmental influences, and personal choices, making it as unique as their physical health.

The Role of Genetics and Epigenetics

Genetics lays the foundation of mental health. Certain individuals inherit a predisposition to specific mental health conditions, just as they might inherit a vulnerability to diabetes or heart disease. However, genes alone don't dictate fate. The concept of epigenetics highlights how environmental factors, such as stress, diet, and exposure to toxins, can switch genes on or off, influencing mental health outcomes. For instance, a child with a genetic predisposition to anxiety might thrive in a nurturing environment but struggle in a chaotic or neglectful one.

The Ecology of the Mind: Home Environment and Caregivers

The mental health of primary caregivers profoundly impacts the developing minds they nurture. Caregivers who exhibit emotional stability, love, and a sense of security create a psychological haven. In contrast, a caregiver struggling with unresolved trauma or emotional instability can inadvertently transfer these burdens to the child. The home environment acts as a mirror, reflecting and shaping the individual's mental stability. A household filled with chaos, constant criticism, or a lack of emotional warmth can hinder a child's ability to develop healthy coping mechanisms.

The Unique Wiring of Every Brain

The human brain is a marvel of individuality. Talents, critical thinking skills, analytical abilities, and emotional intelligence vary widely, even among siblings raised under the same roof. This is because every brain rewires itself based on experiences, learning, and environmental stimuli. The neuroplasticity of the brain allows it to adapt and evolve, but this also means that adverse experiences, such as chronic stress or neglect, can alter its wiring.

The Impact of Environment and Social Dynamics

An environment of chaos or a constant need for validation can shape individuals in profound ways. Some may grow up replicating these patterns, becoming attention-seekers themselves. Others may rebel against these dynamics, seeking peace and solitude. The probabilities of these outcomes, much like physical susceptibility to disease, vary from person to person based on their unique mental framework and resilience.

Mental Health Is Not One-Size-Fits-All

Just as some people are prone to certain illnesses while others remain unaffected, mental health is equally individualized. One person might find solace in solitude, while another thrives in social settings. What soothes one mind might unsettle another. This uniqueness underscores the importance of understanding and respecting individual mental health needs.

Creating a Healthier Mental Landscape

Acknowledging the individuality of mental health is the first step toward fostering it. Here are some ways to promote a nurturing environment for mental well-being:

1. Foster Emotional Security: Create a home environment where feelings are acknowledged and validated.

2. Promote Growth and Resilience: Encourage learning and critical thinking in a supportive setting.

3. Recognize Unique Talents: Celebrate individual strengths and abilities.

4. Address Mental Health Holistically: Consider genetics, upbringing, and environmental factors together.

In conclusion, the mind is as intricate and unique as the body. Understanding this individuality is key to supporting mental health, just as we cater to individual physical health needs. By respecting the distinct wiring of each brain and nurturing it with love, stability, and understanding, we pave the way for healthier minds and, ultimately, a healthier society.

❧

Decluttering mental space

Decluttering your mind is essential for reducing stress, enhancing focus, and achieving clarity. A cluttered mind often results from unprocessed emotions, information overload, and unresolved tasks. Here's a step-by-step approach to clear your mental space:

1. Write It Down (Brain Dump)

Spend 10-15 minutes writing down everything on your mind thoughts, worries, to-dos, or random ideas. This frees up mental space by transferring thoughts from your mind to paper, reducing the mental burden.

2. Prioritize and Organize

Categorize what you've written into actionable tasks, important goals, and things to let go. Prioritizing helps focus on what truly matters while discarding unnecessary worries.

3. Practice Mindfulness

Dedicate time to mindfulness practices like meditation, deep breathing, or yoga. Mindfulness anchors you to the present moment, helping you let go of unproductive thoughts.

4. Set Boundaries with Information

Limit the amount of information you consume daily. Unfollow unnecessary accounts, mute notifications, and avoid endless scrolling on social media. Overexposure to information contributes to mental clutter; simplifying inputs reduces overwhelm.

5. Resolve Unfinished Business

Tackle unresolved tasks and decisions that linger in your mind. Start with small, manageable ones. Unfinished tasks take up mental energy. Completing them creates a sense of accomplishment and clarity.

6. Declutter Your Physical Space

Clean your workspace, home, or any area where you spend significant time. Physical clutter often mirrors mental clutter. A tidy space promotes a clear mind.

7. Focus on Single-Tasking

Avoid multitasking; instead, concentrate fully on one task at a time. Multitasking divides your attention, creating chaos. Single-tasking improves efficiency and reduces mental strain.

8. Practice Gratitude

Reflect on or write down three things you're grateful for each day. Gratitude shifts your focus from worries to positivity, helping to clear mental negativity.

9. Take Regular Breaks

Step away from work, screens, or demanding activities periodically to rest your mind. Breaks recharge your brain and prevent burnout.

10. Say "No" More Often

Politely decline commitments or tasks that don't align with your priorities or capacity. Overcommitting adds unnecessary stress. Saying "no" frees up time and mental energy.

11. Seek Emotional Closure

Address lingering emotions through journaling, therapy, or honest conversations. Suppressed emotions take up mental space. Processing them creates emotional clarity.

12. Sleep Well

Aim for 7-9 hours of quality sleep each night. Sleep clears toxins from the brain and helps process emotions and information effectively.

13. Simplify Your Goals

Focus on a few meaningful goals rather than overwhelming yourself with too many ambitions. A streamlined vision reduces decision fatigue and enhances motivation.

14. Practice Letting Go

Consciously release worries about things you can't control. Holding onto uncontrollable factors drains your mental energy. Letting go fosters peace.

15. Regularly Reflect

Spend time each week reflecting on what's working in your life and what needs adjustment. Reflection ensures you stay aligned with your values and priorities, avoiding unnecessary clutter. By incorporating these practices, you can create a mental environment that's calm, focused, and ready to handle life's challenges effectively.

Insight about perception

The power of perspective lies in its ability to transform not just how you see the world, but how you experience it. A single shift in your mindset can change everything from how you respond to challenges to how you create opportunities. When you realize that your thoughts, beliefs, and actions are interconnected, you unlock the ability to design your life according to your dreams.

How to Embrace a Life by Design:

1. Recognize the Power of Your Mindset

Your beliefs shape your reality. If you believe you're stuck, you will be. If you believe change is possible, it becomes achievable. Start by identifying limiting beliefs and replacing them with empowering ones.

2. Visualize Your Ideal Life

Spend time imagining your perfect life. What does it look like? What are you doing? How do you feel? Visualization activates your subconscious mind to align with your goals.

3. Take Responsibility for Your Choices

Life isn't just about what happens to you; it's about how you respond. Accepting responsibility for your decisions, actions, and attitudes gives you control over your future.

4. Set Clear Goals

Dreaming is the first step, but setting specific, actionable goals turns dreams into reality. Write down your goals and break them into smaller, manageable steps.

5. Practice Gratitude and Positivity

Gratitude shifts your focus from lack to abundance. It rewires your brain to notice opportunities and blessings, fostering a positive outlook.

6. Adapt and Be Resilient

Designing your life doesn't mean avoiding challenges. It means embracing them as opportunities to grow and refine your vision.

7. Surround Yourself with Supportive People

The company you keep influences your mindset. Engage with those who inspire and uplift you, and distance yourself from negativity.

8. Act with Intention

Small, consistent actions lead to monumental changes. Make conscious choices every day that align with your desired life.

When you realize that you hold the pen to your life's story, you step into a position of creative power. You may not control everything, but you can always control your perspective and the actions you take. The journey starts with belief, followed by consistent effort and faith in your vision.

IX
Activities to Include

Here are some worksheets and templates that may be helpful in the healing process of childhood trauma:

Worksheet 1: Identifying Childhood Trauma

1. What are some of the most painful or traumatic experiences from your childhood?

2. How did these experiences make you feel (e.g., scared, sad, angry, ashamed)?

3. How have these experiences affected your life as an adult (e.g., relationships, work, self-esteem)?

Worksheet 2: Understanding the Impact of Trauma

1. How has childhood trauma affected your relationships with others (e.g., trust issues, intimacy issues)?

2. How has childhood trauma affected your self-esteem and confidence?

3. How has childhood trauma affected your emotional regulation and coping mechanisms?

Worksheet 3: Self-Care and Coping Mechanisms

1. What self-care activities make you feel good and help you relax (e.g., exercise, meditation, reading)?

2. What coping mechanisms have you developed to deal with stress and difficult emotions (e.g., journaling, talking to a friend, creative activities)?

3. How can you incorporate more self-care and coping mechanisms into your daily life?

Worksheet 4: Re-Parenting and Self-Compassion

1. What kind of parenting did you receive as a child (e.g., nurturing, neglectful, abusive)?

2. How can you provide yourself with the kind of parenting you needed but didn't receive (e.g., self-compassion, self-care, positive affirmations)?

3. Practice writing a letter to yourself as a child, offering comfort, support, and reassurance.

Worksheet 5: Forgiveness and Letting Go

1. Who or what do you need to forgive in order to move forward (e.g., parents, caregivers, yourself)?

2. What steps can you take to begin the forgiveness process (e.g., writing a letter, talking to a therapist, practicing self-compassion)?

3. How can you let go of negative emotions and memories associated with childhood trauma (e.g., journaling, therapy, creative activities, talking to a friend)?

Worksheet 6: Creating a Safety Plan

1. What are some triggers that can cause you to feel overwhelmed or unsafe (e.g., certain places, people, situations)?

2. What coping mechanisms can you use to manage these triggers (e.g., deep breathing, grounding techniques, reaching out to a support person)?

3. Create a safety plan that includes contact information for support people, coping mechanisms, and self-care activities.

Worksheet 7: Building Resilience

1. What are some strengths and resilience factors that have helped you cope with childhood trauma (e.g., support system, coping mechanisms, self-care activities)?

2. How can you build on these strengths and resilience factors to continue healing and growing (e.g., seeking out new support systems, learning new coping mechanisms, practicing self-care)?

3. What are some goals you have for your healing journey, and how can you break these goals down into smaller, achievable steps?

Template: Trauma Timeline

Create a timeline of your childhood trauma experiences, including:
- Dates or ages when traumatic events occurred
- Description of the traumatic event
- How the event made you feel
- Any coping mechanisms or support systems you used at the time
- How the event has affected your life as an adult

Template: Self-Care Plan

Create a self-care plan that includes:
- Physical self-care activities (e.g., exercise, healthy eating, sleep)
- Emotional self-care activities (e.g., journaling, meditation, spending time in nature)

- Social self-care activities (e.g., spending time with loved ones, joining a social group, volunteering)
- Spiritual self-care activities (e.g., prayer, meditation, connecting with a higher power)
- Creative self-care activities (e.g., art, music, writing)

Template: Safety Plan

Create a safety plan that includes:
- Contact information for support people (e.g., therapist, support group, trusted friends and family)
- Coping mechanisms for managing triggers (e.g., deep breathing, grounding techniques, physical activity)
- Self-care activities for maintaining emotional well-being (e.g., journaling, meditation, spending time in nature)
- Emergency contact information (e.g., crisis hotline, emergency services)

X

6. Mental Agility: Embracing Growth Mindsets

Mental Stability: The Influence of Growth and Fixed Mindsets

Mental stability and success in life are deeply influenced by the mindset an individual adopts. Psychologist Carol Dweck's research highlights two primary mindsets that shape how we view challenges, failures, and potential for improvement: the growth mindset and the fixed mindset. These mindsets not only affect learning and skill development but also play a crucial role in emotional resilience and overall mental health.

The Growth Mindset: A Catalyst for Resilience and Progress

A growth mindset is the belief that abilities and intelligence can be developed through effort, learning, and persistence. People with a growth mindset see failures and obstacles as opportunities to grow rather than as reflections of their inadequacy.

Impact on Mental Stability

1. Resilience to Setbacks: Those with a growth mindset are more likely to recover from failures, viewing them as part of the learning process. This adaptability fosters emotional stability and reduces the risk of long-term stress or anxiety.

2. Self-Belief: Believing in the ability to improve boosts self-esteem and confidence, leading to a more positive outlook on life.

3. Optimism and Problem-Solving: Growth-oriented individuals are solution-focused. They approach problems with curiosity rather than defeat, which enhances mental well-being.

4. Learning from Criticism: Constructive feedback is seen as a tool for improvement, not as a threat to self-worth.

Developing a Growth Mindset

Embrace Challenges: See challenges as opportunities to learn and improve.

Reframe Failures: Instead of focusing on what went wrong, ask, "What can I learn from this?"

Adopt a "Not Yet" Attitude: If success isn't immediate, remind yourself that you haven't succeeded "yet." Progress takes time.

Celebrate Effort: Recognize and reward hard work and persistence, not just outcomes.

The Fixed Mindset: A Barrier to Growth and Stability

In contrast, a fixed mindset is the belief that abilities, intelligence, and talents are innate and unchangeable. This mindset often leads to a fear of failure and an aversion to challenges, as they may expose perceived inadequacies.

Impact on Mental Stability

1. Fear of Failure: Fixed-mindset individuals may avoid risks to protect their self-image, leading to stagnation and missed opportunities.

2. Fragile Self-Worth: Success is tied to external validation. Failures or criticism can severely impact self-esteem.

3. Stress and Anxiety: The pressure to constantly prove oneself can lead to chronic stress, burnout, and feelings of inadequacy.

4. Resistance to Change: A fixed mindset fosters rigidity, making it difficult to adapt to life's inevitable challenges and changes.

Overcoming a Fixed Mindset

Acknowledge Limiting Beliefs: Reflect on areas where you feel stuck and challenge the belief that change isn't possible.

Focus on the Process: Shift attention from outcomes to the learning journey.

Seek Inspiration: Learn from people who have overcome adversity through persistence and effort.

Practice Self-Compassion: Recognize that growth takes time, and setbacks are natural.

Mental Stability Through a Growth Mindset

A growth mindset doesn't just enhance personal and professional success it creates a foundation for mental stability. By embracing change, valuing effort, and viewing setbacks as opportunities, individuals can cultivate resilience, reduce stress, and maintain a balanced perspective in the face of adversity.

On the other hand, the rigidity of a fixed mindset can hinder mental well-being, trapping individuals in cycles of self-doubt and fear. Breaking free from this pattern requires deliberate effort and a willingness to challenge ingrained beliefs.

The Compound Effect of a Growth Mindset

Just as habits accumulate over time to produce significant outcomes, consistently adopting a growth mindset shapes long-term mental health and personal fulfilment. Each small shift in perspective builds on the last, creating a cumulative effect that transforms how we approach life's challenges.

In the end, mental stability is not about avoiding difficulties but about cultivating the resilience to navigate them. The choice to adopt a growth mindset empowers us to harness our potential, embrace life's uncertainties, and thrive both mentally and emotionally.

Fixed Mindset: A Barrier to Growth and Stability

A fixed mindset is characterized by the belief that abilities, intelligence, and talents are static and cannot be improved through effort or learning. This perspective not only limits personal growth but also profoundly impacts mental stability, often leading to emotional stagnation, fear of failure, and a fragile sense of self-worth.

Characteristics of a Fixed Mindset

1. **Avoidance of Challenges**: Challenges are often seen as threats rather than opportunities. A person with a fixed mindset may shy away from difficult tasks to avoid failure.
2. **Focus on Validation**: Success is tied to external approval, making it difficult to pursue intrinsic goals.
3. **Blame and Excuses**: Failure is often rationalized by blaming external factors rather than reflecting on ways to improve.
4. **Rigidity**: There is a strong resistance to change or feedback, as these are perceived as personal criticisms rather than growth opportunities.

Impact on Mental Health and Stability

1. **Increased Anxiety and Stress**: The need to constantly prove oneself creates internal pressure that can lead to chronic stress and anxiety. Individuals may experience a heightened fear of judgment and failure.
2. **Fragile Self-Worth**: When self-worth is tied to outcomes and validation, even minor failures can feel catastrophic, leading to feelings of inadequacy and low self-esteem.
3. **Stagnation and Resentment**: The unwillingness to take risks or learn from failure can result in personal and professional stagnation, fostering resentment toward others who are perceived as more successful or capable.
4. **Negative Feedback Loop**: Avoiding challenges to prevent failure reinforces the belief that growth isn't possible, creating a self-fulfilling prophecy.

Breaking Free from a Fixed Mindset

Shifting from a fixed to a growth mindset is a transformative process, requiring self-awareness, commitment, and deliberate action.

1. **Acknowledge Limiting Beliefs**: Identify areas where you feel "stuck" and challenge the belief that change isn't possible. For instance, instead of thinking, "I'm just not good at this," reframe it as "I'm not good at this yet."
2. **Reframe Failure**: View failure as a learning opportunity rather than a reflection of your worth. Ask yourself, "What can I learn from this experience?"
3. **Seek Constructive Feedback**: Embrace feedback as a tool for improvement rather than a judgment. Recognize that feedback

is about the work, not about you as a person.

4. **Take Small Risks**: Start with manageable challenges that push you slightly outside your comfort zone. Celebrate the effort, regardless of the outcome.

5. **Focus on Effort Over Talent**: Shift your attention to the process of learning and growth rather than innate ability. Understand that progress comes from consistent effort.

The Long-Term Effects of a Fixed Mindset

Without intervention, a fixed mindset can lead to long-term consequences for mental stability:

1. **Chronic Dissatisfaction**: A fixed mindset can create a perpetual sense of unfulfillment, as the individual avoids the growth and challenges necessary for meaningful accomplishments.

2. **Relationship Struggles**: Fear of vulnerability or perceived inadequacy may hinder deep, authentic connections with others.

3. **Career Limitations**: In professional settings, a fixed mindset can prevent individuals from adapting to new roles, learning new skills, or pursuing leadership opportunities.

Transforming Fixed Mindset into Growth Mindset

Moving away from a fixed mindset is not an overnight process, but with consistent effort and self-reflection, transformation is possible.

1. **Start Small**: Focus on one specific area in which you can apply a growth mindset whether it's learning a skill, improving relationships, or managing emotions.

2. **Practice Gratitude**: Acknowledge progress, no matter how small. Gratitude fosters positivity and encourages continued effort.
3. **Build a Support System**: Surround yourself with people who encourage growth and challenge you to step out of your comfort zone.
4. **Develop Emotional Resilience**: Learn to embrace discomfort and uncertainty as part of the growth process.

The fixed mindset traps individuals in a cycle of self-doubt, fear, and stagnation, limiting their potential and undermining their mental stability. Breaking free from its constraints requires courage, persistence, and the willingness to embrace failure as a stepping stone to success.

By transitioning to a growth mindset, individuals can unlock their full potential, build resilience, and cultivate a healthier, more stable mental outlook. The journey may be challenging, but the rewards of personal growth, emotional well-being, and a richer life are well worth the effort.

&

Becoming Strong Amidst Life's Challenges

Regulating your emotions and staying strong in the face of adversity is a journey of self-mastery. It requires a combination of self-awareness, discipline, and resilience. Strength doesn't mean being unaffected by challenges; it means learning to navigate your emotions constructively, keeping your inner balance intact even amidst external chaos. Here's a comprehensive guide to mastering your emotions and building unwavering strength:

1. Understand and Accept Your Emotions

Emotional regulation begins with acknowledging what you feel without judgment. Denial or suppression of emotions only intensifies them over time. Label your emotions: Instead of generalizing, specify: "I feel frustrated," "I feel anxious," or "I feel hurt. Accept them by understanding that emotions are temporary and natural responses to situations. Acceptance helps you gain control over your responses. For instance, feeling anger doesn't mean you have to lash out it's a signal that something needs your attention.

2. Pause Before Reacting

Creating space between your emotions and your actions prevents impulsive, often regrettable, responses. When triggered, pause for a few seconds and breathe deeply. Count to ten or physically step away to cool down. Reflect "Will this matter tomorrow, next week, or in a year?" A pause allows your rational mind to take control, ensuring you respond thoughtfully instead of emotionally escalating the situation.

3. Reframe Negative Situations

Shift your perspective from seeing challenges as setbacks to viewing them as opportunities for growth. Replace "Why is this happening to me?" with "What can I learn from this?" Remind yourself that challenges are temporary and can strengthen your resilience. Reframing helps you focus on growth and improvement, making hardships more manageable and purposeful.

4. Build Emotional Awareness Through Journaling

Writing your thoughts and feelings can help you process emotions and identify triggers. Spend 10 minutes daily journaling about your emotions, triggers, and responses. Reflect on patterns in which situations, people, or environments repeatedly trigger strong emotions. Journaling provides clarity, reduces overwhelm, and helps you develop healthier coping mechanisms.

5. Develop Emotional Resilience Through Habits

Resilience is built by consistently practicing habits that support emotional well-being. Meditate for 5–10 minutes daily to calm your mind and improve emotional awareness. Exercise regularly to release stress and improve mental clarity. Practice gratitude, write down three things you're grateful for each day. Like a muscle, emotional resilience grows stronger with regular practice, helping you bounce back faster from setbacks.

6. Set Boundaries

Protect your peace by limiting exposure to toxic people, draining situations, or unnecessary obligations. Politely but firmly say 'no' to demands that don't align with your well-being. Reduce time spent with individuals who bring negativity into your life. Boundaries protect your energy, allowing you to focus on relationships and activities that uplift and strengthen you.

7. Focus on What You Can Control

Let go of things beyond your control and redirect your energy toward actionable steps. Identify what's within your control, your actions, mindset, and decisions. Release what's not other people's opinions, past mistakes, or external circumstances. Focusing on what you can control reduces stress and gives you a sense of agency and empowerment.

8. Channel Your Emotions Productively

Redirect intense emotions like anger or sadness into healthy, constructive outlets. Engage in physical activities like running, weightlifting, or dancing to release energy. Express yourself creatively like writing, painting, cooking, or pursuing hobbies that calm and inspire you. Productive outlets prevent emotions from festering or manifesting destructively, enabling healthier emotional processing.

9. Strengthen Your Belief in Yourself

Develop an unshakable inner confidence to shield yourself from external negativity. Use daily affirmations: "I am strong," "I can handle this," or "I am enough." Celebrate small wins to reinforce your sense of progress and capability. Belief in yourself builds mental strength, ensuring you remain resilient and self-assured regardless of others' opinions.

10. Ignore External Negativity

Understand that others' judgments or criticisms often reflect their insecurities, not your worth. Remind yourself, "Their words reflect their reality, not mine." Stay focused on your goals, values, and personal growth. By refusing to internalize negativity, you maintain control over your emotional state and self-worth.

11. Embrace Hardship as an Opportunity for Growth

Challenges are inevitable, but you can choose to view them as lessons that build strength. Tell yourself, "This too shall pass" when facing adversity. Reflect on past challenges you've overcome to remind yourself of your resilience. Adversity shapes your character and equips you with the skills to face future difficulties with courage.

12. Surround Yourself with Supportive People

Positive relationships provide encouragement, perspective, and inspiration when life feels tough. Spend time with friends, family, or mentors who uplift and motivate you. Join communities that align with your values and aspirations. A strong support system reinforces your inner strength, offering guidance and reassurance during hard times.

13. Practice Self-Compassion

Treat yourself with kindness and understanding, especially during moments of struggle. Replace self-criticism with encouraging, supportive self-talk. Forgive yourself for your mistakes and focus on what you've learned. Self-compassion nurtures resilience, prevents emotional burnout, and promotes personal growth.

Summary

By cultivating these habits consistently, you can regulate your emotions effectively and build an unshakable fortress of inner strength. Thriving doesn't mean avoiding struggles; it means facing them with grace, resilience, and the confidence that you can overcome whatever life throws at you. True strength lies in mastering yourself, protecting your peace, and choosing growth every step of the way.

Emotional Health – The Operating Environment

XI

7. Understanding Emotional Signals

Understanding Your Emotions: A Journey of Growth and Resilience

Emotions are the essence of our human experience, influencing how we perceive, interact with, and respond to the world around us. Understanding them requires patience, self-awareness, and a willingness to dive deep into the complexities of our inner world. For me, this process begins with writing.

Writing is my tool for introspection. When emotions swell within me whether joy, sadness, anger, or confusion, I put pen to paper or fingers to the keyboard. Writing brings clarity to the chaos in my mind. By transforming intangible feelings into tangible words, I can identify the root causes of my emotions, analyse their patterns, and better understand how they shape my responses.

When I'm broken, I remind myself that I have the strength to rise again. Challenges and pain often bring valuable lessons. Every setback holds the seed of growth if I approach it with an open mind. I reflect on my experiences, dissecting them to find the lessons they offer. Each moment of adversity becomes an opportunity to rebuild myself, stronger and wiser.

I believe in sorting out the system both in my external environment and my internal thought process. If something feels overwhelming, I tackle it piece by piece. I categorize my feelings, identify triggers, and assess my reactions. This process helps me establish a sense of order and empowers me to address problems systematically, rather than being consumed by them.

Life's immunity is built through challenges. Much like our physical immunity strengthens by facing viruses, our emotional and mental resilience grows by encountering and overcoming difficulties. Challenges are the crucibles in which our strength and character are forged. Without them, growth stagnates. They teach us adaptability, patience, and endurance.

In the end, understanding emotions is about embracing them as they are messy and unpredictable, but deeply human. It's about learning, healing, and growing through every experience. By facing our emotions head-on and learning from them, we unlock the power to transform our lives.

While writing is my primary method of understanding my emotions, there are several other approaches I use to deepen my emotional awareness and cultivate resilience. Each method helps me process and grow in unique ways:

1. Reflective Practices: Meditation and Mindfulness

Meditation allows me to sit quietly with my emotions and observe them without judgment. By focusing on my breath and staying present, I create space to notice emotions as they arise. Mindfulness helps me identify emotions in real-time whether it's frustration during a challenging conversation or joy in a fleeting moment. Instead of reacting impulsively, I pause, acknowledge the feeling, and let it guide my actions thoughtfully.

2. Physical Movement

Physical activities like walking, yoga, or even intense workouts have a grounding effect. Movement helps me release pent-up emotions stored in my body. Yoga combines mindful breathing with motion, which helps me process deeper emotions like grief or anxiety. When my mind feels overwhelmed, a brisk walk in nature often clears my head and provides new perspectives.

3. Talking It Out

Sometimes, sharing my feelings with someone I trust like my husband, or a close friend gives me clarity. Verbalizing emotions helps me organize my thoughts and invites external perspectives I might not have considered. A simple conversation can illuminate solutions I hadn't seen or provide the comfort of being heard and validated.

4. Journaling Gratitude and Positivity

Gratitude journaling is another powerful tool. By focusing on what I'm thankful for, even during tough times, I shift my perspective. This doesn't mean ignoring negative emotions but balancing them with recognition of the good in my life. Writing about small victories or moments of joy creates a buffer against overwhelming negativity and builds emotional resilience.

5. Creative Outlets

Engaging in creative activities like cooking, drawing, or crafting helps me channel emotions in a nonverbal way. Creativity allows feelings to flow freely without the constraints of words, often revealing insights I hadn't consciously recognized. Cooking, for instance, becomes a meditative act where I pour love and care into every dish, transforming my emotions into something tangible and nourishing.

6. Learning and Problem-Solving

When emotions stem from a challenge or failure, I turn to learning. Whether it's reading books, listening to podcasts, or seeking guidance, expanding my knowledge gives me tools to address the root causes of my distress. It's empowering to take proactive steps toward growth rather than staying stuck in emotional turbulence.

7. Embracing Solitude

Solitude offers a chance to sit with my emotions without distractions. During these quiet moments, I allow myself to feel full whether it's crying to release sadness or laughing at a memory that brings joy. This self-compassionate practice reminds me that all emotions are valid and temporary.

8. Practicing Self-Compassion

Rather than criticizing myself for feeling "too much" or "too little," I approach my emotions with kindness. I remind myself that it's okay to not have everything figured out immediately. By treating myself as I would a dear friend, I create a safe space to explore my emotions without fear of judgment.

9. Seeking Professional Help When Needed

As a psychologist, I understand the value of therapy and professional guidance. When certain emotions feel too overwhelming or complex, seeking help from a therapist provides a structured and supportive environment to untangle them. Therapy is not a weakness it's a powerful step toward healing and growth.

10. Accepting and Letting Go

Some emotions linger because I resist them or dwell on "what-ifs." Through acceptance, I acknowledge the emotion, process its message, and then let it go. Letting go doesn't mean forgetting; it means releasing the hold an emotion has on me so I can move forward freely.

Incorporating these practices into my life has not only helped me understand my emotions but also built my resilience and emotional intelligence. By using a combination of strategies, I can navigate life's ups and downs with grace, grow through challenges, and nurture a deeper connection with myself and the world around me.

ॐ

Understanding Emotions When Others Put You Down: Rising Above Negativity

When others put you down, it can feel like a direct hit to your sense of self-worth. These moments often trigger deep emotions—hurt, anger, frustration, or even self-doubt. However, I've learned that these experiences, while painful, hold the potential for immense growth and self-realization if approached with the right mindset.

1. Acknowledge Your Feelings Without Judgment

The first step is to validate your emotions. Feeling hurt or upset is natural, and there's no shame in admitting it. Writing about the situation allows me to express these feelings honestly. Through journaling, I often uncover the specific words or actions that affected me most, helping me pinpoint why they had such a strong impact.

2. Separate Their Words from Your Worth

When someone puts you down, their words often say more about them than about you. Recognizing this distinction is crucial. I remind myself that their negativity may stem from insecurity, jealousy, or misunderstandings. My worth isn't determined by someone else's opinion but by the values I live by and the love I give myself.

3. Reflect on Constructive Feedback vs. Baseless Criticism

Not all criticism is harmful. I try to evaluate whether the person's comments hold any constructive insight. If it's valid feedback, I focus on what I can learn from it. If it's baseless or cruel, I remind myself it's not worth dwelling on. Sorting through these layers gives me clarity and direction for improvement while discarding unnecessary negativity.

4. Build Emotional Resilience Through Self-Reflection

Being put down can feel like a loss of control, but I use these moments to regain power through self-reflection. I ask myself: What about this situation made me feel so affected?

Are there unresolved insecurities or fears being triggered?

How can I respond in a way that aligns with my values rather than their negativity?

This process not only strengthens my emotional immunity but also helps me grow from the experience.

5. Respond, Don't React

When faced with negativity, reacting impulsively often escalates the situation. Instead, I choose to pause and respond thoughtfully. Sometimes, silence speaks louder than words; other times, a calm, assertive reply can set boundaries. For example, I might say, "I understand your perspective, but I don't agree with it," to stand firm without engaging in conflict.

6. Surround Yourself with Uplifting People

Negative comments lose their power when you have a supportive circle of friends and loved ones who uplift and affirm you. My husband, for instance, is my constant source of encouragement. Sharing my experiences with those who genuinely care reminds me that one person's negativity doesn't define my worth.

7. Practice Self-Affirmation

Being put down can create doubt, but I counteract this by affirming my strengths and accomplishments. I remind myself of the challenges I've overcome, the love I've shared, and the growth I've achieved. Writing self-affirmations or reciting them daily builds my confidence and shields me from external negativity.

8. Find Strength in Challenges

When someone puts me down, I see it as an opportunity to prove them wrong not out of spite, but to demonstrate my resilience. Every negative comment becomes fuel for my determination to grow, learn, and thrive. Challenges like these are life's way of teaching us to rise stronger.

9. Let Go of the Need for Approval

One of the most liberating lessons I've learned is that not everyone will understand or appreciate me and that's okay. Seeking approval from others gives them power over your happiness. Instead, I focus on living authentically, knowing that my value isn't tied to someone else's opinion.

10. Forgive and Move Forward

Holding onto resentment only prolongs the pain. Forgiving those who put me down doesn't mean condoning their behaviours but rather freeing myself from their influence. Forgiveness allows me to move forward with a lighter heart and an open mind.

Turning Negativity into Growth

Being put down is never easy, but it can become a powerful catalyst for self-discovery and growth. By processing these moments with self-awareness and resilience, I not only understand my emotions better but also emerge stronger and more aligned with my values.

In the end, it's not about what others say but about how you choose to respond, heal, and rise. Life's immunity, after all, is built through challenges—and each challenge you overcome makes you unshakable.

Triggers

How to Identify Your Emotional Triggers: A Step-by-Step Guide

Emotional triggers are powerful reactions to certain situations, people, or memories that evoke intense feelings like anger, sadness, anxiety, or frustration. Recognizing and understanding your triggers is essential for emotional growth and healing. Here's a structured approach to discovering them:

1. Observe Your Reactions

Start by paying attention to your emotions in daily life. Your triggers often surface in moments of strong, seemingly out-of-proportion reactions.

Notice Physical Symptoms: Increased heart rate, sweating, tension, or a "gut reaction" often accompanies emotional triggers.

Track Your Thoughts: Observe what immediately runs through your mind during emotional outbursts or discomfort.

For example, if you feel angry when someone criticizes you, reflect on why that bothers you deeply.

2. Keep a Trigger Journal

Maintaining a journal can help you uncover patterns in your emotional responses. Write down moments when you felt a strong reaction, including what happened, who was involved, and how you felt. Record your thoughts, emotions, and physical sensations during the event. Over time, patterns will emerge in common situations, behaviours, or topics that provoke your emotions.

3. Reflect on Past Experiences

Many emotional triggers stem from unresolved experiences, especially from childhood or past relationships. Reflect on times when you felt powerless, rejected, or hurt. Situations where you felt a need to protect yourself or avoid vulnerability. For instance, if someone's tone of voice bothers you, it could be tied to past experiences of being criticized harshly.

4. Identify Common Trigger Categories

Emotional triggers often fall into these categories:

- Criticism: Feeling attacked or judged.

- Rejection: Fear of abandonment or not being valued.
- Control: Feeling powerless or out of control.
- Neglect: Feeling ignored or dismissed.
- Injustice: Feeling wronged or treated unfairly.

Ask yourself which of these resonates most with your reactions.

5. Notice Your Relationships

Interactions with others can reveal triggers.

- Who do you feel uncomfortable or defensive around?
- What behaviours irritate or hurt you?
- Are there recurring conflicts or misunderstandings in certain relationships?

For instance, feeling triggered by a friend's tone might point to deeper insecurities about acceptance or communication issues.

6. Use Mindfulness to Stay Present

Mindfulness helps you catch triggers as they happen. Practice observing your emotions without judgment. When triggered, pause and ask: What exactly caused this reaction? Notice the gap between the event and your response. This practice helps you identify the specific moment or behaviour that sparked your feelings.

7. Explore Your Beliefs and Expectations

Triggers often arise when situations clash with your core beliefs or unmet expectations. Reflect on:

- Self-Beliefs: Do you believe you're unworthy, inadequate, or unlovable?

- Beliefs About Others: Do you expect people to behave a certain way?
- Cultural or Social Expectations: Do societal norms conflict with your values or experiences?

For instance, if you believe people should always respect your time, being ignored might trigger feelings of disrespect or worthlessness.

8. Seek Feedback from Trusted People

Sometimes, others notice your patterns more clearly. Ask close friends, family, or a therapist to share observations about your emotional reactions. Discuss recurring issues they've noticed in your relationships or behaviour. Hearing others' perspectives can provide valuable insights you may not have recognized.

9. Reflect on "Why" After the Reaction

After an emotional outburst or reaction, ask yourself reflective questions:

- What exactly upset me?
- Was my reaction proportionate to the situation?
- Does this situation remind me of something from my past?
- What need or fear was triggered?

This post-reaction analysis often uncovers the root cause of your emotions.

10. Work With a Professional

A therapist or counsellor can guide you in identifying triggers, especially those tied to trauma or deeply buried emotions. Therapy techniques like Cognitive Behavioural Therapy (CBT) or EMDR (Eye

Movement Desensitization and Reprocessing) can help uncover and reframe emotional triggers.

11. Pay Attention to Positive Triggers

Triggers aren't always negative they can also evoke joy, comfort, or nostalgia. Recognizing these can help balance your emotional awareness and show you the environments or behaviours that support your well-being.

12. Be Compassionate with Yourself

Identifying triggers can bring up painful emotions. Practice self-compassion as you explore your emotional landscape. Remind yourself triggers don't define you they're growth opportunities. It's okay to feel vulnerable during this process. Every step you take toward self-awareness strengthens your emotional resilience.

Summary

Finding your emotional triggers is a journey of self-discovery. By observing your reactions, reflecting on your past, and seeking support when needed, you gain the tools to not only understand your emotions but also manage them more effectively. Over time, this awareness fosters emotional balance, healthier relationships, and a stronger sense of self.

XII

8. The Role of Forgiveness

Taking Charge of Your Life: A Personal Journey of Healing and Resilience

Taking charge of your life is a profound act of reclaiming your power, especially after enduring situations where you've felt manipulated, gaslit, or emotionally drained. My journey toward self-empowerment began with the realization that the toxic patterns in my life were not only affecting my mental well-being but also my sense of self.

Recognizing the Problem

My relationship with this family friend began with what seemed like genuine care and concern. In the early stages, she appeared supportive and attentive, which I appreciated. Yet, there was always a lingering gut feeling a quiet voice warning me that something wasn't right. Against my instincts, I chose to ignore it, dismissing it as overthinking.

Over time, her care revealed itself as humiliating kind acts of "help" that came with strings attached, often leaving me feeling small or indebted. Her behaviour began to show signs of control, crossing my boundaries without hesitation, while her strong envy and projections of insecurity clouded every interaction. I tried responding with kindness, hoping to guide the relationship toward understanding and mutual respect, but my efforts were met with resistance. Nothing seemed to work.

The Turning Point

Finally, I made the difficult decision to step away, prioritizing my well-being. What followed was an unexpected storm of misunderstandings among my family members. Her manipulative nature sowed discord, making it nearly impossible for others to see the truth of the situation. No matter how much I tried to explain, my perspective was dismissed.

This period became a significant turning point in my life. It tested my emotional resilience and broke me down in ways I hadn't anticipated. Yet, amidst the pain, it also became a profound teacher. I learned to rebuild myself, piece by piece, cultivating emotional indifference where it was needed and discovering tools to handle difficult, even toxic individuals.

Though the experience left scars, it also gave me strength rooted in self-respect, resilience, and the unshakable knowledge that listening to my intuition is not just important but essential.

Finding the reality

As I rebuilt myself, I began to see the situation with greater clarity. What initially felt like a complete breakdown of my emotional world became the foundation for growth. I realized that her actions were less about me and more about her—her insecurities, her need for control, and her inability to respect boundaries were reflections of her own struggles. But acknowledging this didn't make the hurt any less valid; it just allowed me to let go of the weight of blame I carried.

The misunderstandings within my family were the hardest to endure. It felt isolating to be unheard and misunderstood by those I trusted the most. For a time, I doubted myself, questioning whether I had misjudged the situation. But deep down, I knew my truth. Standing firm in my perspective required courage, especially when it felt like the odds were stacked against me.

Standing firm with my gut

Through this experience, I also learned the value of setting boundaries not just with people like her but even with my loved ones. I realized that explaining myself repeatedly to those unwilling to listen only drained my energy. Instead, I began to protect my peace by limiting how much I let others' opinions influence my sense of self.

It wasn't an easy journey. There were days when I felt shattered, but with each step, I discovered pieces of myself I had forgotten existed. I found strength in journaling, solace in the love of those who truly supported me, and resilience in the quiet moments when I chose to put myself first.

This chapter of my life has taught me some of the most profound lessons: to trust my intuition, to stand firm in my truth even when it feels lonely, and to understand that not every relationship is meant to last. Some people come into our lives as lessons, and while their presence may bring pain, it also brings growth.

Let the healing begin.

Now, as I look back, I am grateful for the emotional armour I've built. I've learned to handle difficult people with grace but also to walk away when needed. This experience didn't just change me it shaped me into a more self-aware, resilient, and grounded version of myself.

My healing process wasn't linear, nor was it quick. I tried multiple methods of journaling, therapy, and meditation but the real shift happened when I joined Isha Inner Engineering. It was here that I discovered the essence of taking responsibility for my emotions. I realized that by holding myself accountable for how I feel, I could stop allowing others to control my mental state.

Immunity to Negativity

The teachings of Inner Engineering helped me understand that emotions, like any external influences, only hold power when I let them. I learned to observe the subtle rage and narcissistic tendencies of others without internalizing them. Over time, I became immune to their manipulations. This immunity wasn't about becoming indifferent but about prioritizing my inner peace over external chaos.

The Beauty of Letting Go

Initially, severing ties with toxic individuals was painful. There was a sense of loss, betrayal, and even guilt. But as time passed, I realized that these were necessary steps toward freedom. Letting go created space for positivity and growth. What once seemed like a trap was a gift—a way to free myself from what didn't belong in my life.

Reflection as a Psychologist

As a psychologist, I've observed that miserable people often project their internal struggles onto others. Their inability to confront their pain leads them to sabotage relationships. Understanding this has allowed me to view such individuals with compassion rather than anger. While I've chosen not to engage with them, I no longer carry the emotional burden of their actions.

Moving Forward

Taking charge of my life has been a journey of self-awareness, resilience, and conscious effort. Today, I focus on nurturing my mental health, practicing gratitude, and building meaningful relationships. This process has taught me that when I prioritize my well-being, I not only heal myself but also create a ripple effect of positivity around me.

For anyone going through a similar struggle, remember it's okay to outgrow relationships that stifle your growth. It's okay to set boundaries and say no. Most importantly, it's okay to take charge of your life, one step at a time.

Cultivating Inner Strength

One of the most powerful lessons I learned during this journey is the importance of inner strength. The world is full of situations and people who may challenge your peace, but it's not about controlling them it's about mastering yourself. When I began to center my attention on my growth, the power dynamics shifted. I was no longer giving away my energy to defend, explain, or prove myself to others.

Through practices like meditation, mindfulness, and journaling, I developed the ability to pause and respond rather than react. This newfound clarity allowed me to see manipulation for what truly reflected the other person's insecurities. Their attempts to control or provoke me became futile as I built an emotional barrier grounded in self-awareness.

Embracing Responsibility

Taking charge of your life means embracing responsibility not just for your actions but also for your emotions. This doesn't mean blaming yourself for how others treat you. Instead, it's about recognizing that you have the power to choose your reactions.

When I let go of the need to retaliate or seek validation, I felt a profound sense of liberation. I came to understand that my peace didn't depend on others acknowledging their wrongs or changing their behaviour. It depended solely on me deciding what I would allow to affect me.

The Gift of Detachment

Detachment doesn't mean you stop caring it means you stop being controlled by things outside your influence. I learned to detach from toxic people, situations, and even my ego-driven need to be understood or validated by them. This allowed me to create emotional distance while still maintaining compassion.

As I let go of the relationships that no longer served me, I made room for healthier connections. My focus shifted from fixing others to nurturing myself. This shift not only improved my well-being but also set an example for my family and children about the importance of self-respect and boundaries.

Transforming Pain into Power

Every challenge I faced every moment of doubt, hurt, and betrayal became a stepping stone toward a stronger, more empowered version of myself. I stopped viewing setbacks as failures and started seeing them as opportunities for growth.

One of the most freeing realizations was that the toxic people in my life were my greatest teachers. They forced me to confront my own patterns of over-giving, my fear of confrontation, and my tendency to prioritize others at my own expense. In overcoming these, I reclaimed my life.

A Life of Intentionality

Today, my life is guided by intentionality. I am deliberate about how I spend my time, whom I let into my inner circle, and how

I respond to challenges. I choose joy, peace, and self-respect over drama, conflict, and negativity.

Taking charge of your life is not a one-time decision; it's a daily practice. Some days are harder than others, but every small step adds up. When you prioritize your mental and emotional health, you realize that no external force has the power to break you unless you allow it.

A Message of Hope

For anyone struggling with similar challenges, know this you are stronger than you think. The journey may be painful, but it is worth it. Healing is not about erasing the past; it's about transforming it into a source of strength.

Your life is yours to design. When you take charge when you stop waiting for others to change and start changing yourself you unlock a power that no one can take away. You become the author of your own story, and that is the ultimate freedom.

Navigating Triggers with Grace

Even as I grew stronger and more resilient, there were moments when old triggers surfaced moments when a word, an action, or even a memory threatened to pull me back into a cycle of pain. These experiences taught me that healing doesn't mean you'll never feel hurt again; it means you'll know how to handle it when it arises.

When I faced these triggers, I reminded myself of a simple truth emotions are temporary. Instead of suppressing or denying what I felt, I allowed myself to sit with it. I let the feelings flow, journaling my thoughts or meditating until I felt the storm subside. Each time I did this, I grew a little stronger and a little less reactive.

One practice that helped immensely was reframing my perspective. I stopped asking, "Why is this happening to me?" and started asking, "What is this teaching me?" This mindset shift turned painful moments into opportunities for growth.

Reclaiming Joy

Taking charge of my life wasn't just about managing pain; it was about rediscovering joy. Toxic relationships and emotional manipulation had dulled my ability to fully experience happiness. By removing those negative influences, I began to reconnect with the things that truly mattered.

I immersed myself in activities that brought me peace and fulfilment writing, cooking, spending quality time with my family, and deepening my spiritual practice. These small but meaningful acts became a daily reminder that I had the power to create a life filled with purpose and contentment.

As a psychologist, I also channelled my experiences into helping others. Sharing my journey with others and guiding them toward their healing became a source of immense joy and pride. I realized that my pain wasn't just a burden it was a bridge to understanding and supporting others on their paths.

Setting Boundaries with Confidence

One of the most transformative aspects of taking charge of my life was learning to set boundaries. This wasn't easy at first, I worried about being perceived as rude, selfish, or difficult. But over time, I understood that boundaries are an act of self-respect.

I began to communicate my needs clearly and assertively, without guilt or fear. I let go of the need to explain myself or seek approval. This not only protected my energy but also attracted healthier, more respectful relationships into my life.

Celebrating the Journey

Looking back, I can see how far I've come. The person I am today is a testament to the strength I didn't know I had. While the road was rocky, every step was worth it. I've learned to value myself, trust my instincts, and embrace life with open arms.

This journey taught me that we all have the power to take charge of our lives, no matter how lost or broken we may feel. The key is to start small, choose one thing you can do today to honor yourself, and build from there. Over time, these small acts of self-love will add up, and you'll find yourself living a life that reflects your true worth.

Moving Forward with Purpose

The journey doesn't end here. Healing is a lifelong process, and I'm committed to continuing this work not just for myself but for my family, my friends, and anyone who might find inspiration in my story.

Every day is a new opportunity to grow, to learn, and to create a life that aligns with my values. Taking charge of my life isn't just about overcoming the past it's about building a future full of hope, resilience, and unshakable inner peace.

If you're reading this and feel stuck, know that you have the strength to rise above whatever is holding you back. Take the first step, no matter how small, and trust that the path will reveal itself as you walk it.

XIII

9. Cultivating Emotional Intelligence

How to Build Strong Emotional Intelligence

Emotional intelligence (EI) is the ability to recognize, understand, manage, and influence emotions both in yourself and others. Developing strong EI can lead to better relationships, improved decision-making, and greater resilience. Here's a comprehensive guide to building emotional intelligence:

1. Develop Self-Awareness

Self-awareness is the foundation of emotional intelligence. It involves understanding your emotions, triggers, and behaviours. Spend time identifying your emotions during the day. Ask, "What am I feeling and why?" Write about your thoughts, feelings, and experiences to uncover patterns in your emotional responses. Ask trusted friends or family for their observations about your emotional reactions and behaviour.

2. Practice Self-Regulation

Self-regulation helps you manage your emotions effectively, so they don't control your actions. Take a few deep breaths or count to ten when you feel triggered. This helps you respond thoughtfully rather than impulsively. Challenge unhelpful beliefs or assumptions that fuel strong emotions. For instance, replace "They ignored me on purpose" with "They might be busy or distracted. Channel emotions into positive activities like exercise, art, or meditation.

3. Build Empathy

Empathy is the ability to understand and share the feelings of others. Focus on what others are saying without planning your response. Pay attention to their words, tone, and body language. Show genuine curiosity about other people's feelings or perspectives. For example, ask, "How did that make you feel?" Imagine yourself in someone else's shoes to better understand their emotions or reactions.

4. Enhance Social Skills

Strong social skills help you navigate relationships and communicate effectively. Express your thoughts and emotions honestly but respectfully. For example, use "I" statements like "I feel hurt when..." instead of blaming others. Pay attention to facial expressions, tone of voice, and body language to understand unspoken emotions. Approach conflicts calmly, listen to all perspectives, and seek mutually beneficial solutions.

5. Increase Emotional Resilience

Resilience allows you to bounce back from setbacks and stay emotionally balanced. View difficulties as opportunities to learn and grow. Focus on solutions and maintain a positive outlook, even during tough times. Surround yourself with people who uplift and inspire you.

6. Practice Mindfulness

Mindfulness helps you stay present and aware of your emotions without judgment. Spend a few minutes focusing on your breath or observing your thoughts. Check in with how your body feels, as physical sensations often reflect emotional states. Practice mindfulness in daily tasks like eating, walking, or journaling.

7. Learn Emotional Vocabulary

Expanding your emotional vocabulary helps you articulate your feelings and understand others better. Use words that go beyond basic emotions like happy, sad, or angry. For example: Instead of "angry," try irritated, frustrated, or enraged. Instead of "happy," try content, elated, or grateful. This nuanced understanding enhances emotional awareness.

8. Reflect and Learn from Experiences

Every emotional situation is an opportunity to grow. After emotional encounters, ask yourself, "What triggered this? How could I have handled it better?" Reflect on what each experience teaches you about yourself and others.

9. Stay Open to Feedback

Feedback, especially about emotional interactions, is invaluable for growth. View feedback as an opportunity to improve rather than a personal attack. Actively seek input from mentors, colleagues, or loved ones about how you handle emotions and relationships.

10. Practice Gratitude and Positivity

Focusing on the positive helps you manage emotions and build better connections. Keep a Gratitude Journal that lists things you're thankful for each day. Acknowledge your own and others' accomplishments, big or small.

11. Build Emotional Boundaries

Healthy boundaries protect your emotional well-being. Politely decline requests that overwhelm you or violate your values. Communicate what behaviours are acceptable in relationships.

12. Continuously Educate Yourself

Emotional intelligence is a lifelong journey. Explore books like Emotional Intelligence 2.0 by Travis Bradberry or The Gifts of Imperfection by Brené Brown. Join courses on emotional intelligence, communication, or leadership. Incorporate small EI practices into your routine to keep growing.

Key insight

Building strong emotional intelligence takes time, practice, and self-compassion. By committing to self-awareness, empathy, and mindful interactions, you can navigate emotions more effectively, strengthen relationships, and lead a more balanced, fulfilling life.

Mastering Emotional Independence: Finding Inner Peace Amid Chaos and Toxic Interactions

Life is a tapestry of connections and experiences, many of which can uplift and nurture us. Yet, there are moments when we encounter chaos, toxic relationships, and behaviours that test our emotional resilience. While external challenges are inevitable, we possess the power to cultivate an unshakable inner peace a sanctuary within that remains undisturbed by external turmoil. Mastering emotional independence is about setting boundaries, building self-awareness, and fostering resilience to thrive amidst life's storms.

Here's a detailed guide to help you navigate this journey:

1. Choose Inner Peace Over External Validation

Inner peace begins with a choice: the decision to prioritize your well-being over the need for external validation or control. External turmoil, whether in the form of toxic behavior or unpredictable circumstances, often tempts us to react emotionally. Recognizing that you control your reactions is the first step toward emotional independence.

Peace isn't determined by circumstances; it is a state of mind. Toxic behaviours often thrive on provoking reactions. By detaching from the need to fix or justify these behaviour's, you reclaim your emotional power. Focus on understanding your own emotions instead of trying to decode or change others. This shift empowers you to stay grounded in your truth, regardless of external negativity.

2. Set Boundaries That Empower

Boundaries are essential for emotional well-being. They serve as protective barriers, shielding you from draining interactions and helping you define what you will and won't tolerate in your life. Without clear boundaries, toxic people can easily manipulate, overstep, and drain your energy.

Boundaries create a safe emotional space for you to nurture your peace. Politely but firmly decline requests or behaviours that feel intrusive or harmful. Visualize an emotional "shield" around yourself, reinforcing that others' negativity cannot penetrate your inner sanctuary.

3. Practice Detached Compassion

Detachment doesn't mean becoming cold or indifferent; it's about maintaining emotional distance from others' behaviours and actions. Often, toxic individuals act out of their insecurities and struggles. Understanding this allows you to engage with compassion while preserving your peace.

Toxic behaviour is rarely about you; it's a reflection of the other person's internal battles. Accepting this helps you avoid taking their actions personally. Reframe toxic behaviours as symptoms of their struggles rather than as attacks on you. Offer empathy from a safe emotional distance without feeling the need to solve their problems.

4. Use Mindfulness as a Shield

Mindfulness anchors you in the present moment, allowing you to remain calm and centred even amidst chaos. By focusing on the "now," mindfulness reduces the mental clutter that toxic interactions often create. Toxic environments often provoke stress and overthinking. Mindfulness breaks the cycle by helping you focus on what you can control—your present thoughts and actions.

Practice deep breathing to calm your nervous system during stressful moments. Observe your emotions and thoughts without judgment, gaining clarity instead of reacting impulsively. Engage in grounding exercises, like focusing on physical sensations, to stay present and composed.

5. Respond Intentionally, Not Emotionally

Toxic individuals often provoke impulsive reactions to manipulate or control situations. Mastering the art of pausing before responding can neutralize their power. Emotional reactions often escalate conflicts, giving toxic individuals the control they seek. Thoughtful responses, on the other hand, diffuse tension and assert your emotional independence.

Take a deep breath before replying to manipulative or provocative remarks. Use Silence Strategically: Not every statement requires a response. Silence can be a powerful way to disarm negativity. Choose Assertive Language, respond calmly and confidently, avoiding aggression or passivity.

6. Cultivate Emotional Self-Awareness

Self-awareness is the foundation of emotional resilience. By understanding your triggers, patterns, and vulnerabilities, you become less susceptible to manipulation and more confident in managing your emotions. Toxic people often exploit unresolved wounds or insecurities. Self-awareness helps you identify and heal these areas, making you less vulnerable to their tactics.

Reflect on how toxic behaviours affect you and why they trigger certain emotions. Own your feelings, acknowledging them as valid without letting them dictate your actions. Seek professional support or self-help resources to address unresolved emotional wounds.

7. Create Inner Sanctuaries for Peace

Even amid chaos, you can cultivate moments of peace by creating a sanctuary a mental or physical space where you can recharge and reflect. A sanctuary provides a refuge from external noise, reminding you that peace is always accessible within.

Designate a quiet, calming space at home for activities like journaling, meditation, or reading. Visualize a mental sanctuary during stressful moments, imagining a peaceful, safe place where you can retreat. Incorporate calming rituals, such as lighting candles, listening to soothing music, or walking in nature.

8. Foster Gratitude to Reframe Negativity

Gratitude is a powerful tool for shifting focus from what's draining you to what's uplifting you. It rewires your brain to find joy and strength, even in challenging situations. Focusing on abundance rather than lack fosters emotional resilience and reduces the impact of negativity.

Keep a gratitude journal, listing things you're thankful for each day. Reframe hardships as opportunities for growth and self-discovery. Celebrate small wins, like maintaining composure in a difficult interaction.

9. Recognize When to Walk Away

Sometimes, the best way to preserve inner peace is to disengage from toxic relationships entirely. Letting go doesn't mean failure; it's an act of self-respect. Continuously exposing yourself to toxic behaviour can erode your emotional health. Walking away prioritizes your well-being over harmful connections.

Assess the relationship's impact on your mental and emotional health. Gradually reduce interactions with toxic individuals. Seek support from friends, family, or professionals as you distance yourself.

10. Redefine Peace as Inner Strength

True peace isn't about avoiding challenges or toxic individuals; it's about standing tall and calm amidst them. It's a practice of resilience, self-awareness, and intentionality. Peace isn't a constant state but a skill you cultivate over time. Each moment of composure and clarity strengthens your emotional independence.

Embrace your growth by acknowledging progress, no matter how small. Let go of the pursuit of perfection; instead, focus on returning to peace whenever it's disrupted. Celebrate your resilience, knowing you have the power to thrive despite external chaos.

Summary

Mastering emotional independence is a lifelong journey of self-discovery and empowerment. You reclaim your emotional power by choosing peace, setting boundaries, and cultivating mindfulness. Toxic interactions and chaos lose their grip when you anchor yourself in resilience and self-awareness. Remember, the greatest sanctuary lies within, and no external force can disrupt the peace you cultivate for yourself.

Spiritual Health – The Power Source

XIV

10. The Soul's Compass: Connecting with Your True Self

The Soul Compass: True Connection

The Soul Compass is a powerful metaphorical guide designed to help individuals navigate their inner world, rediscover their authentic selves, and align with their deepest truths. It represents the intuitive pull within each of us, guiding our decisions, emotions, and sense of purpose in life. Unlike an external compass that points north, the Soul Compass is deeply personal and constantly recalibrating based on our experiences, values, and spiritual journey.

What Is the Soul Compass?

At its core, the Soul Compass symbolizes the innate wisdom that resides within. It's the voice of intuition, the whisper of clarity amidst chaos, and the steady pulse of your true essence. When life feels overwhelming or unclear, the Soul Compass serves as a tool to reconnect with who you truly are, beneath societal expectations and external influences.

The Need for a Soul Compass

In a fast-paced, distraction-filled world, it's easy to lose sight of our authentic selves. Social conditioning, responsibilities, and unprocessed emotions can cloud our sense of direction, leading to feelings of disconnection, burnout, or emptiness. The Soul Compass provides a way back to an inner anchor that ensures our choices resonate with our purpose and values.

Connecting with Your True Self Through the Soul Compass

1. Listening to Your Inner Voice

The first step to connecting with your Soul Compass is cultivating mindfulness. Through practices like meditation, journaling, or simply sitting in stillness, you can quiet the noise of the external world and tune in to your inner voice. This is where the truth of your desires, fears, and dreams resides.

2. Clarifying Your Values

Like a compass relies on magnetic north, the Soul Compass aligns with your core values. Reflect on what truly matters to your family, freedom, creativity, and compassion, and use these as your guiding stars.

3. Releasing External Expectations

To fully connect with your Soul Compass, it's crucial to let go of the need to meet others' expectations. This means embracing your imperfections, setting boundaries, and making peace with the idea that you cannot please everyone.

4. Practicing Self-Awareness

Regular self-check-ins are essential to keep your Soul Compass calibrated. Pay attention to your emotions, energy levels, and physical sensations, as they often indicate whether you're aligned with your true self.

5. Embracing Change

Life is ever-evolving, and so is your Soul Compass. As you grow and learn, your inner guidance may shift. Trust this process and embrace change as a natural part of your journey.

Benefits of Connecting with Your Soul Compass

Inner Peace: By aligning with your true self, you cultivate a profound sense of calm and contentment.

Purposeful Living: Every decision feels more intentional, paving the way for a life of meaning and fulfilment.

Authentic Relationships: When you're true to yourself, you attract relationships that nurture and support your growth.

Resilience: The Soul Compass gives you the strength to navigate challenges with grace and clarity.

Exercises to Strengthen Your Connection

Morning Journaling Prompt: "What does my inner self need from me today?"

Meditation Visualization: Imagine holding a compass in your hands. What direction does it guide you toward?

Daily Alignment Check: At the end of each day, ask yourself, "Did I honour my true self today?"

The Soul Compass is a profound yet simple tool for connecting with your true self. It reminds you that the answers you seek are already within, waiting to be uncovered. By trusting this inner guidance, you can move through life with a sense of purpose, peace, and authenticity.

Authenticity

Authenticity is the foundation of wholeness. It means embracing the truth of who you are, without masks or pretences, and living in alignment with your core values and beliefs. In a world that constantly pushes you to conform to external expectations, authenticity requires courage—a willingness to stand in your truth, even when it feels vulnerable or uncomfortable.

When you are authentic, you stop seeking validation from others and start finding fulfilment within. You no longer feel the need to fit into predefined roles or meet societal standards that don't resonate with your heart. Instead, you define your own path, guided by your inner voice. Authenticity empowers you to own your story the triumphs and the struggles—without shame or fear of judgment.

Living authentically also deepens your relationships. When you show up as your true self, you invite others to do the same. This openness fosters trust, connection, and genuine intimacy. You no longer rely on external approval to feel valued because your sense of worth comes from within. This shift creates space for healthier, more meaningful relationships that are rooted in mutual respect and understanding.

However, authenticity is not static; it evolves as you grow and learn. It requires continuous self-reflection and a willingness to confront uncomfortable truths about yourself. It means being honest about your needs, boundaries, and aspirations, even when it challenges the status quo. Authenticity demands that you let go of the fear of rejection and embrace the freedom that comes from being unapologetically you.

To live authentically, you must also cultivate self-compassion. Accepting yourself means acknowledging that you are a work in progress. It's about embracing your flaws, learning from your mistakes, and celebrating your unique strengths. When you stop trying to be perfect, you allow yourself to be real and that realness is where your true power lies.

In the journey of wholeness, authenticity is the bridge between your inner and outer worlds. It aligns your thoughts, words, and actions, creating harmony in every aspect of your life. By being authentic, you unlock the potential to live with purpose, passion, and peace. You become a beacon of truth, inspiring others to embark on their own journey of self-discovery and transformation.

Authenticity is not just a choice; it's a practice. Each day offers opportunities to reconnect with your true self and honour your unique path. It's in this practice of authenticity that you find the freedom to live fully and love deeply, as the person you were always meant to be.

Authenticity is the essence of living a fulfiled and meaningful life. It is the process of peeling back the layers of conditioning, societal expectations, and self-imposed limitations to reveal the truest version of yourself. When you embrace authenticity, you honour your individuality and recognize that your worth is not tied to external achievements or the approval of others—it is intrinsic and undeniable.

To be authentic means to live in harmony with your values and beliefs, making choices that align with your truth rather than what others expect of you. It is a journey of self-awareness, requiring you to reflect on who you are, what you stand for, and what brings you joy and purpose. Authenticity isn't about being rigid; it's about being honest with yourself, even as your values and priorities evolve.

One of the most liberating aspects of authenticity is the freedom it brings. When you stop pretending to be someone you're not, you release the heavy burden of maintaining facades. You no longer feel the need to hide your imperfections or compare yourself to others. Instead, you find peace in embracing your uniqueness, recognizing that your flaws and quirks are what make you human and relatable.

Authenticity also fosters resilience. When you live in alignment with your true self, you develop a stronger sense of self-worth and inner stability. External criticism or setbacks no longer shake you because your foundation is rooted in self-acceptance. You learn to trust yourself, to listen to your intuition, and to make decisions that feel right for you, even if they go against the grain.

In relationships, authenticity is transformative. It allows you to connect with others on a deeper level because you are no longer hiding behind a mask. Authenticity invites vulnerability, which is the cornerstone of trust and intimacy. When you show up as your true self, you create space for others to do the same, leading to more meaningful and fulfilling connections.

However, being authentic is not without challenges. It often requires unlearning patterns of people-pleasing or perfectionism that have been ingrained over time. It may mean setting boundaries, saying no to what doesn't serve you, and facing the discomfort of standing out or being misunderstood. But these challenges are worth it because they lead to a life that feels real and fulfilling—a life that is truly your own.

Authenticity is also about grace and self-compassion. It's recognizing that you don't have to have it all figured out or get everything right. Being authentic doesn't mean you'll never falter; it means you'll own your mistakes, learn from them, and keep moving forward with integrity.

Ultimately, authenticity is an act of self-love. It's a declaration that you are enough, just as you are. By embracing your authentic self, you unlock your potential to live a life of purpose, passion, and profound joy. It's in the embrace of your truth that you discover not only who you are but also the limitless possibilities of who you can become.

XV
Techniques to Introduce

Finding Serenity in the Storm: My Journey with Zen Meditation

As I sit here, reflecting on my experiences with Zen meditation, I am transported back to my early twenties. It was a time of discovery, growth, and transformation. I had stumbled upon this ancient practice, which would become a cornerstone of my spiritual journey.

I remember the first time I sat in stillness, surrounded by the cacophony of everyday life. The sounds of the environment, the chirping of birds, the rustling of leaves, and the distant hum of traffic were a symphony of distractions. Yet, I was determined to quiet my mind and listen.

The instruction was simple: sit comfortably, close your eyes, and focus on the sounds around you. Don't try to identify them; hear them. Whenever thoughts arose, acknowledge them and let them drift away like clouds in the sky. Don't engage; simply observe.

At first, my mind was a restless monkey, jumping from thought to thought. But as I persisted, something remarkable happened. My thoughts began to slow, and my attention became more focused. I was no longer a slave to my wandering mind.

The benefits of Zen meditation were profound. I could concentrate more intensely, shutting out distractions and immersing myself in the task. I was no longer at the mercy of my environment; I had learned to cultivate inner peace amidst chaos.

This newfound calm had a ripple effect on my life. I became more resilient and better equipped to handle life's challenges. I was no longer easily rattled by noise, stress, or uncertainty. I had discovered a deep well of inner strength, a sense of stability that remained unshaken regardless of external circumstances.

As I continued this path, I found that I could meditate anywhere, anytime. Whether in a quiet forest glade or amidst the hustle and bustle of city life, I could retreat into my inner sanctuary, finding peace and clarity amid the turmoil.

Looking back, I realize that Zen meditation was more than just a practice – it was a way of life. It taught me to appreciate the beauty of simplicity, to find joy in the present moment, and to cultivate compassion for myself and others.

If you're seeking a deeper sense of calm, clarity, and purpose, I encourage you to explore the world of Zen meditation. It may just become your sanctuary, a source of strength and inspiration that will stay with you for the rest of your life.

ॐ

Cultivating Stillness of the Mind Through Meditation

Achieving stillness of the mind is one of the most transformative benefits of meditation, but it requires practice, patience, and a compassionate approach to yourself. The mind is naturally restless, and attempting to force it into stillness often backfires. Instead, creating a supportive environment and practicing intentional techniques can help you work toward a calm, focused state. Here's how:

1. Set the Stage for Meditation

Creating the right environment is essential for stillness. Find a location where you're unlikely to be interrupted. Soft lighting and a clutter-free setting help create a calming atmosphere. Meditate when your mind is less active, such as early morning or before bed. Sit in a comfortable position yet keep your alert. Use cushions or a chair if needed to prevent physical discomfort.

2. Start With the Breath

Your breath is the anchor to stillness. Start by focusing on the natural rhythm of your breathing. Take slow, deep breaths, inhaling through your nose and exhaling through your mouth. Pay attention to the sensation of air entering and leaving your body. If your mind wanders, gently return your focus to your breath without frustration. The simplicity of this practice helps ground your mind and body.

3. Accept the Presence of Thoughts

It's normal for the mind to wander, especially when you're starting. Instead of trying to suppress your thoughts. Acknowledge them without judgment. Imagine your thoughts as clouds drifting by observe them, but don't hold onto them. Return your focus to your breath, a mantra, or a visualization. Stillness comes not from eliminating thoughts but from detaching from them.

4. Use Guided Meditations

If maintaining focus feels challenging, guided meditations can help. These typically include soothing instructions or imagery that direct your mind gently. Apps like Calm, Headspace, or Insight Timer offer options for beginners and seasoned meditators alike.

5. Introduce a Mantra or Affirmation

Repeating a mantra (a word or phrase) silently or aloud can help centre your mind. Choose something simple, like "Peace," "I am calm," or a Sanskrit mantra like "Om Shanti" (peace). Focus on the sound or meaning of the mantra as you repeat it. This repetitive focus helps quiet mental chatter.

6. Embrace Body Awareness

Engage in a body scan meditation to connect with the present moment. Bring your attention to each part of your body, starting from the top of your head and moving to your toes. Notice sensations like tension or relaxation. Release any stress as you move through each area. This practice grounds you in the present, fostering stillness.

7. Practice Mindful Observation

If sitting meditation feels too daunting, start with mindful observation. Focus on an object, like a candle flame, Diya, or a flower. Observe its details colour, texture, or movement. Allow your mind to rest on the object, bringing it back if it strays. This practice helps train your mind to concentrate without force.

8. Cultivate Patience and Consistency

Stillness doesn't happen overnight. It's a gradual process that requires consistent effort. Start small with 5–10 minutes a day, gradually increasing the time. Celebrate small victories, like a few moments of stillness during a session. Be patient with yourself restlessness is part of the journey.

9. Incorporate Movement Meditations

Stillness doesn't have to mean sitting still. Practices like yoga, tai chi, or mindful walking combine gentle movement with meditation, helping restless minds ease into focus. As you move, synchronize your breath with your motions to stay present.

10. Reflect After Each Session

After meditating, take a moment to reflect on how you feel. Did you notice moments of calm or clarity? Were there recurring thoughts or emotions? This reflection deepens your understanding of your mind and enhances future sessions.

11. Seek Guidance and Support

If you find meditation challenging, consider joining a meditation group or attending a class. Working with a teacher who can offer personalized guidance. Sharing the journey with others can motivate and deepen your practice.

12. Trust the Process

True stillness isn't about silencing the mind completely it's about creating space between your thoughts and your awareness. Over time, meditation helps you develop this awareness, teaching you to observe without reacting.

As you continue practicing, you'll notice subtle shifts; a quieter mind, a greater sense of peace, and the ability to approach life with clarity and calm. Stillness is not a destination but a journey one that transforms you in profound ways.

Visualization, affirmation, and manifestation prompt

Here's a set of affirmations and manifestation prompts tailored for cultivating a strong, resilient mind and emotional peace. You can recite these in the morning or before bed:

Morning Manifestations for Strength and Peace

1. "I am capable, calm, and in control. Today, I embrace every challenge with courage and grace."

2. "I am the architect of my thoughts. I choose positivity, resilience, and inner peace."

3. "Every situation I face is an opportunity to grow stronger and wiser."

4. "I trust myself to handle whatever comes my way. My mind is powerful, and my heart is open."

5. "I release fear and invite calmness into my life. I am a force of strength and serenity."

Evening Manifestations for Emotional Peace

1. "I release all stress and tension. My mind is calm, and my heart is at peace."

2. "Every experience today has shaped me into a stronger, more mindful person."

3. "I forgive myself and others, freeing my soul from the weight of negativity."

4. "I am grateful for my journey and the lessons it brings. Peace flows through me as I rest."

5. "I trust in the universe's plan and let go of all that no longer serves me."

Manifestation Visualization (Optional Add-on)

Close your eyes and imagine yourself as an unshakable tree, with deep roots anchoring you to the earth. No matter how strong the winds of life blow, you remain steady and grounded, with your leaves dancing gracefully. Visualize peace and strength radiating from within.

Here's an expanded version with more affirmations to repeat and visualize for building a strong, resilient mind and emotional peace:

Morning Manifestations for Strength and Positivity

1. "I am the creator of my reality. Today, I choose strength, clarity, and joy."

2. "My mind is my ally, and I train it to focus on solutions, not problems."

3. "I am resilient like a mountain. I stand firm, no matter what life brings."

4. "I am in tune with my emotions, and I choose to respond with calm and wisdom."

5. "I attract peace and positivity into my life with every breath I take."

Evening Manifestations for Peace and Growth

1. "I release all doubts and worries as the day ends. My heart is light, and my mind is free."

2. "I acknowledge my challenges and celebrate my progress. I am growing every day."

3. "My past does not define me. I am grateful for my strength to rise above."

4. "I invite healing, forgiveness, and love into my life as I rest."

5. "I am ready to embrace tomorrow with strength, peace, and unwavering determination."

Visualization Prompts for Deep Emotional Peace

Imagine a serene lake within you. Even if stones (challenges) are thrown, the ripples settle, and the water becomes calm again. Let your inner peace reflect this stillness.

Picture yourself surrounded by a golden light that protects you from negativity. With every inhale, the light grows brighter; with every exhale, it pushes stress and fear away.

Visualize your challenges as stepping stones in a river. See yourself crossing them with confidence, knowing each step brings you closer to a stronger, more fulfilled version of yourself.

Affirmations for Becoming a Better Person

1. "I am kind, compassionate, and open to growth. I treat myself and others with love and respect."

2. "I embrace my imperfections as a part of my unique journey. They guide me to become better."

3. "I am grateful for the lessons life teaches me. I use them to grow wiser and stronger."

4. "I radiate positivity, peace, and strength to those around me."

5. "I am a continuous work in progress, striving every day to live authentically and beautifully."

Recite these with intention, visualize the outcomes, and watch your inner strength and emotional balance flourish!

Here are affirmations and manifestation prompts focused on embracing your uniqueness and feeling deeply connected to the universe:

Morning Manifestations: Embracing Uniqueness and Universal Connection

1. "I am a one-of-a-kind creation, and my uniqueness is my strength."

2. "I embrace who I am, knowing that my individuality adds beauty to the world."

3. "I am a part of the infinite universe, connected to its endless wisdom and energy."

4. "My existence has purpose and meaning, and I trust the flow of life to guide me."

5. "I am aligned with the universe, and I trust its timing for my journey."

Evening Manifestations: Celebrating Your Connection to the Universe

1. "I release the need to compare myself to others. I am unique, and that is my superpower."

2. "I honour my place in the universe, knowing I am a vital part of its harmony."

3. "I am grateful for the infinite possibilities that the universe offers me each day."

4. "The universe supports me, and I trust in its divine plan for my life."

5. "As I rest, I connect deeply with the universe, absorbing its peace and energy."

Visualization Prompts for Embracing Uniqueness

1. Imagine yourself as a star in a vast galaxy, shining brightly in your unique light. Each star has its place, and your light is an essential part of the cosmos.

2. Picture yourself as a flower in a meadow. No two flowers are the same, yet each contributes to the meadow's beauty. See your uniqueness as a vital part of the world's tapestry.

3. Visualize a deep, glowing connection between you and the universe—a golden thread linking your heart to the stars, the earth, and all living beings. Feel the energy of oneness flowing through you.

Affirmations for Celebrating Individuality and Universal Connection

1. "I am proud of my individuality; it is what makes me extraordinary."

2. "I am not separate from the universe; I am a beautiful part of its infinite design."

3. "I honour my journey, trusting that the universe unfolds in perfect harmony for me."

4. "I release the fear of judgment. My uniqueness is my gift to the world."

5. "I feel the love, wisdom, and support of the universe in every breath I take."

These affirmations can help you embrace your individuality while feeling deeply connected to the vastness of existence.

XVI

11. Practices for Inner Peace

Self-discovery is a deeply personal journey, and while journaling is a powerful tool, it's not the only way to find yourself. People can explore their inner selves through various practices and experiences that resonate with their personalities, interests, and lifestyles. Here are some alternative approaches to self-discovery for finding inner peace in your journey of life.

1. Meditation and Mindfulness

Quieting the mind through meditation allows individuals to observe their thoughts without judgment. Mindfulness practices help people stay present and become more aware of their emotions, reactions, and desires. Guided meditations or mindfulness exercises can be particularly helpful for beginners.

2. Creative Expression

Art, music, dance, or writing stories can help people express emotions and thoughts they may not fully understand. Creativity often uncovers hidden passions and aspects of one's personality. Trying new creative hobbies can spark inspiration and lead to unexpected self-discoveries.

3. Engaging in Nature

Spending time in nature can provide clarity and perspective. Activities like hiking, gardening, or simply sitting in a park encourage reflection and a sense of connection to the world. Nature often has a calming effect, allowing for deeper introspection.

4. Reading and Learning

Books, especially those focused on personal growth, philosophy, or biographies, can provide insights into one's values and goals. Learning a new skill or subject can reveal talents and interests one didn't know existed.

5. Travel and Exploration

Exploring new places exposes individuals to different cultures, lifestyles, and perspectives. Travel challenges comfort zones, fosters independence, and often leads to moments of introspection and self-awareness.

6. Therapy or Counselling

Talking to a trained therapist or counsellor provides a safe space to explore thoughts, emotions, and experiences. Professional guidance can help individuals uncover patterns and overcome obstacles to self-understanding.

7. Physical Activity

Activities like yoga, martial arts, or even running help connect the mind and body. Physical movement can clear mental clutter and provide a space for introspection.

8. Social Interactions

Building relationships and engaging in meaningful conversations can reveal aspects of one's personality, strengths, and values. Surrounding oneself with people who inspire, and challenge personal growth can also be transformative.

9. Volunteering or Acts of Service

Helping others can provide a sense of purpose and highlight what truly matters to an individual. It's an opportunity to discover strengths, passions, and causes that resonate deeply.

10. Self-Reflection Through Questions

Asking oneself deep questions like What are my core values? What brings me joy? What do I want my legacy to be? Can guide self-discovery. Practices like gratitude exercises or keeping a vision board can also aid reflection.

11. Experimenting with New Experiences

Trying new activities or stepping out of one's comfort zone often reveals hidden capabilities and interests. Whether it's taking up a new sport, joining a club, or starting a passion project, these experiences help define identity.

12. Dream Analysis

Dreams often reflect subconscious thoughts, fears, and desires. Keeping a dream log or reflecting on recurring themes can provide insights into unresolved emotions or hidden aspirations. Exploring symbolism in dreams can help individuals connect with their deeper selves.

13. Practicing Gratitude

Regularly reflecting on what you're grateful for can shift focus from external validation to internal fulfilment. Gratitude practices often reveal what truly matters and what aligns with your values.

14. Facing Challenges and Adversity

Life's difficulties can often be catalysts for self-discovery. Overcoming challenges helps people understand their strengths, resilience, and coping mechanisms. Reflecting on how you handle adversity can teach important lessons about your character and priorities.

15. Personality and Strengths Assessments

Tools like the Myers-Briggs Type Indicator (MBTI), Enneagram, or StrengthsFinder can provide insights into your personality traits, strengths, and preferences. While these tests aren't definitive, they often serve as a starting point for self-reflection.

16. Practicing Minimalism

Simplifying life by focusing on essentials can clarify priorities and values. Letting go of material or emotional clutter often helps people identify what truly brings happiness and meaning.

17. Reflection After Significant Events

Major life changes like starting a new job, ending a relationship, or becoming a parent often prompt a revaluation of identity and goals. Taking time to reflect on these transitions can lead to profound self-awareness.

18. Daily Affirmations and Visualization

Positive affirmations can reshape limiting beliefs and encourage a deeper understanding of one's potential. Visualization of goals and dreams provides clarity on what truly matters and motivates action toward personal growth.

19. Joining Communities or Groups

Engaging with like-minded people in book clubs, support groups, or spiritual circles can foster self-awareness through shared experiences and mutual learning. Group discussions often bring new perspectives that deepen understanding of oneself.

20. Seeking Feedback from Trusted People

Honest and constructive feedback from people you trust can reveal blind spots in your personality or behaviour. While external opinions should never define you, they can offer valuable perspectives for reflection.

21. Practicing Self-Compassion

Self-discovery requires kindness toward yourself. Accepting imperfections and celebrating small wins helps you uncover your authentic self without judgment. Engaging in self-care rituals whether it's taking a long bath, reading, or meditating allows you to reconnect with your needs and feelings.

22. Spiritual Practices

For some, spiritual activities like prayer, attending religious gatherings, or studying sacred texts deepen their understanding of life's purpose and their place within it. These practices often provide a framework for introspection and connection to something greater than oneself.

23. Listening to Music or Podcasts

Certain songs, lyrics, or podcast discussions can resonate deeply, triggering self-reflection or sparking realizations about personal values and beliefs. Curating playlists that align with your moods can also help you connect with your emotions.

24. Mindful Observation of Daily Habits

Noticing how you spend your time, react to situations, or make decisions can reveal much about your priorities and values. Tracking habits over time can help identify patterns that support or hinder personal growth.

25. Documenting Achievements and Failures

Maintaining a record of accomplishments and setbacks provides insight into what drives and challenges you. Reflecting on these moments can help you better understand your motivations, strengths, and areas for improvement.

Ultimately, self-discovery is an ongoing process that evolves with time and experience. Whether it's through introspection, external feedback, or engaging in new experiences, the journey is unique to every individual. The key is to remain open, curious, and compassionate with yourself as you uncover the many layers of who you are which helps you to attain inner peace whenever you are in chaos.

XVII

12. The Interconnectedness of All Things

The Interconnectedness of Health

Life is an intricate tapestry woven from the threads of physical, mental, emotional, and spiritual health. Each of these dimensions, though distinct, forms a part of the whole, interdependent and deeply intertwined. A truly happy and fulfilled life emerges when harmony exists among these dimensions, much like a symphony where every instrument plays in tune. When one aspect falters, it creates ripples that disrupt the balance, causing dissonance in the broader symphony of life.

Physical health is the foundation upon which all other forms of well-being rest. A strong and nourished body supports the mind and spirit, enabling us to engage fully with life's challenges and joys. Conversely, neglecting physical health can lead to fatigue, chronic illnesses, or pain, which in turn clouds the mind and dampens the spirit. Regular exercise, balanced nutrition, and adequate rest are not just acts of self-care but essential investments in maintaining this foundation.

Mental health is the powerhouse of resilience and clarity. It shapes how we perceive the world and respond to it. A sound mind can navigate the complexities of life with poise, fostering rational thinking and effective decision-making. However, when mental health is strained, even the strongest physical health can feel burdensome. Anxiety, stress, or depression can weigh heavily on the spirit, causing a cascading effect on emotional well-being and physical vitality. Thus, nurturing mental health through mindfulness, therapy, or meaningful intellectual pursuits is vital.

Emotional health forms the connective tissue between our internal world and the external environment. It governs our relationships, responses, and sense of empathy. Emotional wounds, when left unhealed, can manifest as bitterness or detachment, affecting not only our connections with others but also our inner peace. Recognizing and expressing emotions authentically whether through art, journaling, or open communication is crucial in fostering emotional resilience and a sense of belonging.

Finally, spiritual health is the anchor that provides a sense of purpose and direction. It transcends religious practices and touches upon our deeper values, beliefs, and sense of connection to something greater than ourselves. Spiritual well-being cultivates hope, gratitude, and a sense of unity, which can uplift the mind, heal emotional scars, and even enhance physical recovery. When spiritual health is neglected, life can feel hollow, leading to existential crises that shake the foundations of all other dimensions.

These dimensions of health do not exist in silos but interact dynamically. Poor physical health can strain the mind and spirit; unresolved emotional turmoil can weaken the body and cloud the soul; and a lack of spiritual grounding can leave us vulnerable to mental and emotional instability. Conversely, strengthening one dimension often reinforces the others. For instance, engaging in physical exercise can elevate mood and foster mental clarity, while meditative practices can enhance emotional and spiritual resilience.

A harmonious life, therefore, is one where these four dimensions coexist in balance. This balance does not imply perfection but rather a conscious effort to nurture each dimension with equal care. Just as a gardener tends to a variety of plants, each requiring different nourishment, so too must we tend to the different aspects of our health. Only then can we create a life that is not just functional but flourishing a life that radiates happiness, fulfilment, and a deep sense of interconnectedness.

Choosing Resilience: A Reflection on My Journey

Growing up, my life revolved around the love and wisdom of my grandparents. My grandfather, a Tamil Pulavar, had an extraordinary story he ran away from his family and marriage at the tender age of 13 to pursue education and became a respected teacher. My grandmother, though quieter in her expressions, radiated immense love and compassion, nurturing everyone in her unique, understated way. Together, they built a home filled with empathy and understanding, which became my sanctuary amidst the chaos of my early life.

My mother, a teacher by profession, often seemed weighed down by her responsibilities. Her frustration and unhappiness stemmed from both her job and her tumultuous relationship with my father. Their dysfunctional marriage was marked by daily arguments, leaving a lasting impact on me as a child. Despite this, my mother often visited us at my grandparents' home, seeking solace in the compassionate atmosphere they created. It was only during my college years that we discovered my mother had schizophrenia. This diagnosis explained much of her erratic behaviour and inner struggles. While medication has brought some stability, her happiness remains elusive a reality that deeply shapes my perspective on mental health and life's challenges.

Witnessing two contrasting family dynamics my grandparents' harmonious bond and my parents' turbulent relationship was both enlightening and challenging. It taught me the importance of choosing happiness and resilience over succumbing to misery. My childhood was far from easy. Between the emotional toll of my mother's condition and instances of being mistreated by relatives, I often felt vulnerable and unsafe. These experiences shaped my sense of self and instilled in me a deep understanding of boundaries. I consciously avoided environments and people where I felt disrespected or unsafe, focusing instead on my personal growth and inner strength.

Through it all, I refused to let my circumstances define me. Instead of blaming situations or people, I directed my energy toward building myself up. I learned to see adversity as a person, one that revealed the depth of my resilience and the value of self-reliance. This perspective has made me acutely aware of the divide between those who grow up in comfort and those who navigate life's harsher realities. People raised in comfort often struggle to grasp the weight of challenges faced by those in difficult circumstances. But for me, every hardship became an opportunity to choose joy and purpose over despair.

Today, as I reflect on my journey, I feel a profound gratitude for the strength I've cultivated and the love I've received from my grandparents. Their unwavering support laid the foundation for my ability to rise above adversity. Life has taught me that happiness is not a passive state; it is an active choice. Despite a childhood marked by emotional upheaval, I stand resilient, determined to create a life defined not by my past, but by the hope and strength I choose every day.

This journey has also shaped my empathy and understanding of human complexities. Living with a mother who battles schizophrenia has taught me to see beyond the surface, to recognize the silent struggles people endure. It has instilled in me a deeper sense of patience and compassion. I understand now that mental illness is not a flaw but a challenge that requires understanding and support. My mother's resilience, despite her unhappiness, is a testament to her strength, and I honour her for continuing to fight her battles.

However, my childhood also made me hyper-aware of the importance of self-preservation. While I empathize with others' struggles, I have learned to prioritize my emotional well-being. Growing up in an environment where some relatives crossed boundaries or disrespected me, I realized early on that safety both physical and emotional was not something to compromise. By avoiding people and places where I felt unsafe or unvalued, I reclaimed my power. This decision to distance myself from toxic situations wasn't easy, but it was necessary for my growth.

I often reflect on the stark differences between my grandparents' compassionate bond and my parents' discord. These contrasting dynamics served as a mirror, helping me understand what I want in life and what I need to avoid. My grandparents taught me the power of mutual respect, love, and a life rooted in values. Their example reminds me that even in a world filled with challenges, we can create spaces of peace and understanding.

This philosophy has guided me through adulthood. I now believe that happiness is a choice a deliberate act of prioritizing one's well-being, even when the odds seem insurmountable. Choosing happiness does not mean ignoring pain or challenges; it means acknowledging them while refusing to let them define your story. It's about finding small moments of joy and nurturing them into something bigger.

I also realize that I carry the weight of my family's struggles, but I choose to see it as a gift rather than a burden. It has given me a unique perspective on resilience and taught me the value of self-awareness. I believe that people who have faced hardships often develop a profound sense of empathy and wisdom that cannot be learned in comfort. My experiences have not made me bitter; they have made me stronger, kinder, and more determined to create a life that reflects my values.

Looking back, I am grateful for the lessons my life has taught me. My journey has been far from perfect, but it has been meaningful. I have learned to embrace my imperfections and celebrate my progress, no matter how small. I have also learned to let go of anger, of blame, of anything that does not serve my growth.

Moving forward, I aim to live with purpose and continue to prioritize my happiness. I want to create a life filled with love, respect, and compassion not just for myself but for those around me. I want to honour the lessons of my grandparents by cultivating relationships that are rooted in mutual understanding. Above all, I want to continue growing, learning, and choosing joy, no matter what challenges come my way.

This is my story, not of survival alone, but of thriving despite the odds. It's a story of choosing light over darkness, hope over despair, and happiness over misery. It's a testament to the fact that no matter where we come from or what we endure, we have the power to rewrite our narrative and build a life that we are proud of.

XVIII
Insights to Share

Path of my Journaling

Journaling has been a transformative journey for me, helping me keep my emotions in check and navigate life's complexities. It started simply writing about my thoughts and feelings, a casual practice I committed to during a 100-day writing challenge. Although I missed days here and there, I didn't let it discourage me. I wrote without pressure, and over time, I realized how profoundly it impacted me.

As an introvert, I often find it difficult to openly express my likes, dislikes, or emotions. Growing up in an environment where I avoided asking for or demanding things, I became flexible and adaptable to various situations. However, journaling gave me a voice a safe space where I could vent, reflect, and understand myself better.

Through this process, I learned to prioritize my emotional and mental well-being. Journaling taught me to recognize what I truly need and set boundaries. I no longer tolerate situations or people that drain my peace; instead, I protect my energy and prioritize my family, which is the heart of my life. Writing helped me see this it became not just a practice but a lifestyle.

A major part of this journey is the respect and support I receive from my husband. He understands how sacred my journaling is and respects my privacy, never intruding on my notebooks. This mutual respect for boundaries strengthens our relationship. I respect his professional space, and he respects my need to write, which creates harmony in our lives.

Journaling has not only helped me balance my emotions but also deepened my self-faith and spiritual well-being. It's my tool to reflect on what I can control, what I want from life, and how to navigate challenges. Life throws its share of hardships, but I no longer get frustrated or overwhelmed by others' behaviour. Writing keeps me grounded and helps me embrace each day as an opportunity to grow.

Through this practice, I've blossomed into a person who blooms like a butterfly every day resilient, evolving, and at peace with herself. Journaling is more than an outlet; it's my guide to becoming the best version of myself.

Journaling has become a mirror reflecting my inner world and showing me who I truly am. It has helped me break free from the expectations and judgments that often weigh us down. When I put my thoughts on paper, I see patterns in my behaviour, emotions, and decisions. I understand the reasons behind my feelings and actions, and this clarity allows me to grow stronger and more self-aware.

One of the most beautiful aspects of this journey is how it has shaped my relationship with myself. Writing has taught me to be gentle with my flaws and celebrate my strengths. I no longer see mistakes as failures but as stepping stones to becoming wiser. Each entry in my journal is a testament to my resilience a story of overcoming challenges, however small or big they may be.

Journaling also empowers me to set boundaries in relationships. It has given me the courage to walk away from people or situations that disturb my peace. This isn't always easy, but the sense of liberation it brings is worth it. Protecting my mental health has become non-negotiable, and my journal reminds me of why this is important.

Spiritually, journaling has been a gateway to mindfulness and gratitude. By reflecting on my day, I've learned to focus on what truly matters my family, my passions, and my inner harmony. Even on difficult days, when life feels overwhelming, my journal is a space where I can process my thoughts and find a glimmer of hope. It reminds me that every storm passes, and I have the strength to weather it.

The most heartwarming realization through journaling has been the discovery of my priorities my son, daughter, and my family. Writing has shown me how deeply I cherish being present for them and nurturing their growth. It's a joy to document our little moments together and revisit them later, seeing how much we've grown.

As I write, I feel a sense of renewal. It's as if each word I put down frees me from the clutter of the day, leaving me lighter and more focused. My journal has become my sanctuary, my confidant, and my guide. It's a tool that helps me align my emotions, thoughts, and actions, ensuring that I live intentionally and authentically.

Journaling is not just about documenting my life; it's about creating it with intention. It's where I find meaning, strength, and clarity. It's where I bloom, one page at a time.

Importance of it in self-discovery

Journaling has been a cornerstone of my journey toward self-discovery. It's not just a practice of writing it's a deliberate act of meeting myself on the page, uncovering layers of my identity, and understanding who I truly am. Each time I write, I delve deeper into my thoughts, feelings, and beliefs, often uncovering aspects of myself I wasn't fully aware of.

In the process of journaling, I've learned to listen to my inner voice the one that often gets drowned out by the noise of daily life. It has helped me differentiate between what society expects of me and what I genuinely desire. Through this practice, I've discovered my passions, values, and boundaries. I've realized what makes me happy, what triggers me, and what I need to thrive emotionally and mentally.

Self-discovery through journaling is like peeling back layers of an onion. Some entries are light and surface-level, while others dig deep into the core of my being. On difficult days, writing becomes a mirror, reflecting fears or insecurities I may have been avoiding. By confronting them on paper, I learn to understand, accept, and work through them. This process has been instrumental in cultivating self-compassion, helping me embrace my imperfections as part of my humanity.

Journaling also provides clarity about the roles I play in life as a mother, a wife, a friend, and most importantly, as an individual. It has helped me rediscover dreams I thought I had let go of and uncover new aspirations I didn't know I had. Writing about my experiences allows me to see patterns, recognize my growth, and make intentional choices moving forward.

Perhaps the most profound aspect of journaling in self-discovery is the sense of empowerment it brings. When I write, I take control of my narrative. I'm no longer a passive observer of my life; I'm an active participant, shaping my story with awareness and purpose. It has taught me to be honest with myself and has shown me the beauty of authenticity.

Journaling reminds me that self-discovery is not a destination but a continuous journey. It's about evolving, learning, and embracing the person I am becoming every day. Through this practice, I've found a deeper connection with myself and a clearer understanding of what makes my life meaningful. It's a powerful tool that keeps guiding me toward becoming the best version of myself.

❧

Interconnections: Linking the Parts of the Human System

XIX

13. Bridging Physical and Mental Health

The Inseparable Dance of Body and Mind

The connection between physical and mental health is an undeniable and intricate dance, where the condition of one profoundly influences the other. Understanding this interplay is key to fostering holistic well-being, as it allows us to address the root causes of ailments rather than treating symptoms in isolation.

The Mutual Influence of Physical and Mental Health

Physical health forms the foundation of our mental resilience. When the body thrives, it creates fertile ground for a sound mind. Conversely, mental well-being acts as the anchor for physical vitality, driving healthy behaviours and physiological balance. Yet, this relationship is not always harmonious. Challenges in one domain often ripple into the other, creating cycles of distress that are difficult to break.

Consider the role of physical activity. Exercise has long been heralded as a remedy for anxiety and depression. Aerobic activities like running or swimming release endorphins chemicals in the brain that act as natural mood lifters. Exercise also reduces levels of the body's stress hormones, such as adrenaline and cortisol, fostering a calmer mental state. The physical act of movement serves not only to tone muscles but also to ease the mind, illustrating the profound link between the two realms.

Now, imagine a contrasting scenario: chronic illness. Conditions like diabetes or arthritis demand relentless physical and emotional energy. The toll of pain, limited mobility, or medical regimens often leads to feelings of frustration, hopelessness, and depression. The mental strain exacerbates physical symptoms, creating a feedback loop that can be challenging to disrupt.

The Biological Pathways Connecting Body and Mind

This interplay is not simply anecdotal it is deeply rooted in biology. Stress, for example, activates the hypothalamic-pituitary-adrenal (HPA) axis, a system that controls the release of cortisol. While cortisol helps the body manage acute stress, prolonged activation of the HPA axis can lead to immune suppression, digestive disturbances, and even heart disease. Similarly, stress-induced neurochemical changes can disrupt serotonin levels, contributing to mood disorders.

Mental health conditions like anxiety can also manifest physically. A racing heart, tense muscles, or irritable bowel syndrome are common physiological expressions of mental distress. These symptoms highlight the duality of our experiences: what affects the mind inevitably affects the body.

The Role of Psychosocial Factors

Beyond biology, psychosocial elements bridge physical and mental health. Social support, for example, acts as a buffer against stress, reducing its physiological impact. A strong sense of purpose and connectedness can inspire healthier behaviors, from better nutrition to consistent physical activity. Conversely, social isolation and stigma especially in chronic illness or mental health disorders can compound physical symptoms and delay recovery.

Practical Strategies for Holistic Well-Being

To address this interconnectedness, an integrated approach to healthcare is essential. Here are some practical strategies:

1. Promote Regular Physical Activity: Incorporate movement into daily routines. Activities like yoga, tai chi, or even walking can balance the mind and body by reducing stress and enhancing overall health.

2. Foster Stress Management: Techniques such as mindfulness meditation, deep breathing, and cognitive-behavioral therapy (CBT) can help regulate the HPA axis and support mental clarity.

3. Encourage Balanced Nutrition: A nutrient-rich diet supports both physical energy and brain function, enhancing mood stability and resilience.

4. Seek Integrated Care: Collaboration between mental health professionals and primary care providers can create a comprehensive treatment plan addressing both physical and psychological needs.

5. Nurture Social Connections: Build and maintain a supportive network of family, friends, or community groups to strengthen emotional and physical health.

The human system thrives on the synergy between physical and mental health. Recognizing their interdependence allows us to adopt a more compassionate and effective approach to well-being. By fostering this balance through integrated care, informed practices, and mindful living, we can ensure that the dance of body and mind remains harmonious and sustaining for a lifetime.

ಌ

Image of Gut

The gut, primarily the large intestine, is home to trillions of unique microbiotas that play a crucial role in our overall health. Often referred to as the "second brain," the gut communicates directly with the central nervous system (CNS) through a sophisticated network called the brain-gut axis. This connection impacts not just our physical health but also our mental well-being.

Each bacterium in the gut has a symbiotic relationship with us. While some bacteria promote health, others can be detrimental depending largely on our dietary choices. The power to nurture beneficial bacteria and suppress harmful ones lies in our hands.

By embracing a disciplined diet, one rich in vegetables and proteins with moderate carbs we can avoid many chronic diseases. A balanced approach, such as a 90% natural and wholesome diet complemented by 10% indulgence for cravings, can lead to a healthier lifestyle. After all, our gut health reflects our energy, mood, and overall well-being.

Dos for Good Gut Health

1. Dietary Fiber

Fruits, vegetables, and greens are vital for gut health as they are rich in dietary fiber, which acts as a prebiotic food for gut bacteria. While macronutrients like carbohydrates, proteins, and fats are digested in the stomach and absorbed in the small intestine, fiber remains undigested and reaches the large intestine, where it nourishes gut microbes.

2. Fermented Foods

Fermented foods are a gut health treasure. South Indian staples like idli and dosa, along with global favorites like kimchi, sauerkraut, curd, cheese, and overnight millet porridge, are packed with probiotics. These natural probiotics replenish gut bacteria and enhance digestion. However, artificially fermented products or commercial drinks may not survive the stomach's acidic environment as effectively.

3. Sleep and Exercise

Sleep is essential for gut health. During restful sleep, the gut microbiota regenerate and support overall body repair. Midnight snacking or heavy dinners disrupt this process. Exercise, too, contributes to a healthy gut by releasing beneficial gut-derived chemicals that bolster immunity and metabolism.

Don'ts for Gut Health

1. Excess Sugar

Sugar, whether processed or natural, spikes blood glucose levels, providing no nutritional value and harming gut health. Overconsumption can lead to sugar addiction, which not only disrupts gut balance but also paves the way for diseases like diabetes, hypertension, and obesity.

2. Unchecked Cravings

Cravings often arise from glucose spikes, creating a vicious cycle of overindulgence. Studies suggest early sugar addiction can increase susceptibility similar to nicotine addiction later in life.

3. Ultra-Processed Foods

Ultra-processed food canned, packed, and ready-to-eat products are laden with chemicals, preservatives, and stabilizers that harm gut bacteria. Long-term consumption of such foods can trigger inflammation, gut dysbiosis, and serious health issues.

The Gut-Brain Connection: How Gut Health Influences Mental Health and Emotional Well-Being

The relationship between gut health and mental well-being is increasingly recognized in scientific research. Known as the gut-brain axis, this complex connection involves direct and indirect communication between the gut and the brain through the nervous system, hormones, and immune pathways. Here's how a healthy gut can significantly impact your mental and emotional state:

1. The Gut is the "Second Brain"

The gut contains the enteric nervous system (ENS), a network of about 100 million neurons embedded in its walls. This "second brain" doesn't control thought or decision-making but regulates digestion and communicates with the brain. This connection explains why gut disturbances are often linked to mood changes, anxiety, or even depression.

2. Role of the Microbiota

Trillions of gut microbes play a pivotal role in mental health. These microbes produce neurotransmitters, Gut bacteria synthesize serotonin (often called the "happiness hormone"), dopamine, and gamma-aminobutyric acid (GABA), which regulate mood, sleep, and anxiety levels. About 90% of the body's serotonin is produced in the gut. Modulate stress response, Balanced gut bacteria reduce cortisol levels, the primary stress hormone, improving resilience to stress.

Chronic gut inflammation can lead to neuroinflammation, contributing to mental health issues like depression and anxiety.

3. Gut and Emotional Well-Being

A healthy gut fosters emotional balance by, reducing stress. When the gut is healthy, the vagus nerves a key part of the gut-brain axis send calming signals to the brain, reducing stress and promoting relaxation. Enhancing focus and clarity a nourished gut supports better concentration and cognitive function. Microbiota balance influences melatonin production, ensuring better sleep, which is critical for emotional well-being.

4. Mental Health Disorders and Gut Imbalances

Emerging studies reveal links between gut imbalances and various mental health issues. People with depression often have less diverse gut bacteria. Probiotics and prebiotics have shown promise in alleviating depressive symptoms. Research suggests that altered gut microbiota may influence behavioural symptoms in individuals with autism. Chronic stress can disrupt the gut lining, leading to a "leaky gut," which exacerbates inflammation and mental health issues.

Improving Mental Health Through Gut Care

1. Probiotic and Prebiotic Foods: Incorporate fermented foods (curd, kimchi, sauerkraut) and high-fibre foods (greens, whole grains) to nourish gut bacteria.

2. Avoid Ultra-Processed Foods: These disrupt the microbiota, negatively impacting mood and focus.

3. Manage Stress: Mindfulness, yoga, and meditation can strengthen the gut-brain connection by reducing stress.

4. Stay Active: Exercise releases beneficial gut-friendly compounds that enhance mood and reduce anxiety.

5. Prioritize Sleep: Adequate rest supports both gut regeneration and emotional stability.

The Power of the Gut-Brain Axis in Emotional Regulation

The gut-brain axis plays a significant role in how we process emotions, regulate mood, and respond to stress. Understanding this connection can empower you to make lifestyle choices that not only benefit physical health but also enhance emotional well-being.

1. Mood Stabilization

The gut's production of serotonin and other neurotransmitters impacts emotional stability. For example, a healthy gut can help regulate emotional highs and lows, reducing feelings of irritability, sadness, or anger. On the other hand, an imbalanced gut microbiota may lead to emotional instability or heightened stress responses.

2. Gut Microbes and Anxiety

When gut health is compromised through poor diet, stress, or illness it can lead to overactivation of the stress response system. This results in increased cortisol levels, which can exacerbate anxiety and reduce your capacity to cope with everyday challenges.

3. Emotional Eating

A disrupted gut can influence cravings and appetite, often leading to emotional eating. Foods rich in sugar and unhealthy fats feed harmful bacteria, creating a cycle of poor gut health and emotional distress. This highlights the importance of mindful eating to support both the gut and emotional balance.

Practical Steps to Align Gut and Mind Health

1. Practice Mindful Eating

Chew food slowly to improve digestion and absorption. Focus on eating a variety of nutrient-dense, fibre-rich foods to promote gut diversity.

2. Incorporate "Mood Foods"

Omega-3 Fatty Acids: Found in fatty fish, flaxseeds, and walnuts, they reduce inflammation and support mental clarity. Probiotic-Rich Foods: Include curd, kefir, or fermented vegetables to boost beneficial gut bacteria. Complex Carbohydrates: Whole grains and legumes provide sustained energy and stabilize mood.

3. Manage Stress Holistically

Meditation and Breathing Exercises: Calm the mind and body, improving gut-brain communication. Regular movement enhances gut motility and the release of feel-good chemicals like endorphins. Emotional expression can reduce stress, indirectly benefiting gut health.

4. Stay Hydrated

Proper hydration is essential for smooth digestion and maintaining a healthy gut lining.

5. Limit Gut Stressors

Avoid excessive caffeine, alcohol, and ultra-processed foods, which can disrupt the gut-brain axis. Practice portion control to avoid overburdening the digestive system.

A Balanced Gut for a Balanced Life

Your gut is like a best friend it thrives with consistent care. A colourful plate filled with greens, fruits, and whole foods promotes glowing skin, improved metabolism, and vibrant energy. Conversely, bad gut bacteria, much like toxic relationships, may seem appealing initially but ultimately deplete your health, leading to fatigue and chronic diseases.

When your gut thrives, so does your mind. You'll notice improved focus, better energy levels, and a calmer demeanour. Small, consistent changes in your diet and lifestyle can lead to profound transformations in your mental and emotional health.

By fostering a healthy gut, you're not just promoting digestion you're creating a foundation for a more joyful, resilient, and emotionally balanced life. Take the first step today, and your gut will reward you with long-lasting harmony between mind, body, and soul.

XX

14. Mental Health as the Key to Emotional Stability

Mental Health: The Pillar of Emotional Stability

Mental health forms the cornerstone of a person's overall well-being, influencing how they think, feel, and behave in daily life. It serves as the key to emotional stability, shaping our ability to cope with stress, build relationships, and make sound decisions. Understanding the importance of mental health is vital in a world where the pace of life often leaves little room for introspection and self-care.

The Role of Mental Health in Emotional Stability

Emotional stability refers to the ability to maintain balance and composure in the face of challenges, setbacks, and changes. It allows individuals to process emotions constructively, respond to situations thoughtfully, and recover from stress or adversity. Mental health underpins this stability, acting as the foundation for resilience and emotional regulation.

When mental health is nurtured, it provides clarity of thought and emotional equilibrium. A person with good mental health can manage stress, empathize with others, and approach life's uncertainties with confidence. Conversely, when mental health is compromised, emotions may become overwhelming, leading to anxiety, irritability, or mood swings that disrupt daily functioning and relationships.

Mental Health and the Brain

The brain plays a central role in maintaining emotional stability. Regions such as the prefrontal cortex and amygdala regulate emotions, decision-making, and stress responses. A healthy mental state supports optimal functioning in these areas, allowing individuals to adapt to challenges without losing composure.

However, mental health conditions like anxiety or depression can alter brain chemistry and structure. For instance, chronic stress can lead to an overactive amygdala, making individuals more prone to fear or anger, while diminishing activity in the prefrontal cortex, which governs rational thinking. These changes can destabilize emotions, leading to cycles of negativity and distress.

The Impact of Mental Health on Everyday Life

The influence of mental health extends far beyond the individual—it affects relationships, work, and physical health. Someone struggling with mental health may find it difficult to communicate effectively, leading to misunderstandings or conflicts. At work, poor mental health can result in decreased productivity, creativity, and decision-making.

Moreover, the mind-body connection means that emotional instability can manifest physically. Symptoms like fatigue, headaches, or weakened immunity often accompany mental health struggles, creating a feedback loop that further impacts emotional stability.

Strategies to Foster Mental Health and Emotional Stability

Achieving emotional stability requires intentional effort to nurture mental health. Here are some strategies:

1. Cultivate Self-Awareness: Regularly reflect on thoughts and emotions through journaling or mindfulness practices. Self-awareness helps identify triggers and patterns, making it easier to manage emotional responses.

2. Practice Emotional Regulation: Techniques such as deep breathing, progressive muscle relaxation, and grounding exercises can help stabilize emotions during stressful situations.

3. Seek Social Support: Building a strong network of family, friends, or support groups fosters emotional resilience by providing a sense of connection and belonging.

4. Prioritize Rest and Recovery: Sleep and relaxation are essential for mental health. Adequate rest allows the brain to process emotions and restore balance.

5. Engage in Therapy or Counselling: Professional guidance from therapists or counsellors can offer tools and insights for managing emotions and maintaining mental health.

6. Adopt a Growth Mindset: Embrace challenges as opportunities for growth. A positive outlook builds resilience and strengthens emotional stability over time.

The Interplay Between Mental Health and Emotional Intelligence

Emotional stability is closely tied to emotional intelligence the ability to understand, manage, and express emotions effectively. Good mental health enhances emotional intelligence, enabling individuals to navigate social complexities and build meaningful relationships. It also empowers them to empathize with others, fostering deeper connections and mutual understanding.

Mental health is not merely an absence of illness; it is the foundation of a balanced and fulfiling life. By prioritizing mental health, individuals can achieve emotional stability, empowering them to face life's challenges with courage and grace. As society continues to evolve, recognizing mental health as a vital aspect of well-being will pave the way for more compassionate, resilient, and emotionally stable communities.

The Abyss of Mental Instability

Mental illness is a shadow that cloaks the mind, often leaving individuals in a tumultuous state where emotions reign supreme, unchecked, and unbalanced. In this storm, control over life becomes a distant dream. The inability to regulate inner chaos fosters profound disconnection, not just from others but also from oneself. This lack of cooperation and understanding stems not from intent but from an internal battle that remains unarticulated and unresolved.

When mental stagnation takes root, life becomes a barren field devoid of growth. The absence of personal evolution traps individuals in cycles of repetitive pain. Joy and peace, the bedrock of human fulfilment, seem inaccessible. Old age, in such cases, becomes an unbearable weight a bitter culmination of unresolved conflicts and regrets. Unhealed wounds ripple outward, affecting not only the individual but also the environment.

In this state of instability, accountability becomes an alien concept. Evading responsibility for actions and words often leads to harmful behaviours and projecting insecurities onto others. This inability to introspect and course-correct perpetuates self-sabotage, a destructive cycle that chains individuals to emotional turmoil. Manipulation, though damaging, becomes a survival mechanism, a desperate attempt to exert control in an uncontrollable world.

The first and hardest step for those struggling with mental instability is acknowledging their struggles. Denial acts as a shield, protecting them from the pain of introspection but also perpetuating dysfunction. Therapy, counselling, and sometimes medical intervention are critical tools for breaking free. These resources help build the skills needed to process emotions, regulate thoughts, and take ownership of actions.

Healing is not linear. Setbacks, frustration, and the temptation to revert to old patterns are inevitable. Change threatens the fragile equilibrium they have maintained. However, with persistence, a support system, and the willingness to confront inner demons, growth becomes possible.

Mental stagnation robs individuals of the chance to experience life's depth and meaning. Without addressing the roots of instability, they risk a life of regret, estranged relationships, and unfulfilled existence. Yet, choosing the path of self-awareness and healing opens the door to possibilities of a life filled with authentic joy, meaningful connections, and peace born from self-understanding.

True transformation begins when individuals take responsibility for their healing, no matter how late they start. It requires courage to step out of the comfort zone of blame and denial and face uncomfortable truths. Self-awareness becomes the cornerstone of this process. Without it, cycles of harm to self and others continue unabated.

Breaking free from mental instability involves recognizing that healing is about progress, not perfection. Small steps, like identifying triggers, learning coping mechanisms, and practicing mindfulness, pave the way for long-term stability. Therapy or counselling provides a safe space to confront suppressed emotions and dismantle harmful patterns. Practices like yoga and meditation foster mental clarity, bridging the mind-body connection.

For those around individuals struggling with instability, understanding while maintaining healthy boundaries is essential. Supporting accountability and independence, refusing to enable harmful behaviours, and prioritizing self-care ensure balance in relationships. True support encourages seeking help and fosters a healthier dynamic.

As healing begins, self-sabotage gives way to growth. Mistakes become lessons, trust is rebuilt, and relationships improve. The void of instability starts to fill with purpose, hope, and connection. Old age, once feared, can transform into a period of wisdom and fulfilment. Addressing mental instability at any stage allows individuals to rewrite their narratives. Scars of the past become symbols of resilience rather than pain.

Mental stability is the foundation of growth. Without it, individuals remain trapped in cycles of emotional turmoil and unfulfilled potential. With courage, effort, and support, rising above chaos becomes possible. The journey is arduous, but the rewards of inner peace, meaningful connections, and a legacy of growth make it worthwhile.

One of the profound consequences of mental instability is the inability to forge genuine emotional connections. Relationships thrive on empathy, understanding, and vulnerability qualities often compromised by inner turmoil. Instead of warmth and openness, individuals may retreat or express emotions erratically.

This lack of connection isolates them from the support and intimacy they crave. Misunderstanding others' feelings, projecting insecurities, or engaging in manipulative behaviours further alienates loved ones. Over time, relationships deteriorate as trust erodes and boundaries are established to protect against harm.

The root of this disconnection lies in an inability to understand one's own emotions. Without processing personal feelings, recognizing or validating others' emotions becomes challenging. Rebuilding emotional intelligence through identifying and regulating emotions, active listening, and cultivating empathy is essential. Journaling, therapy, and open conversations bridge internal and external worlds, fostering connection.

Healing and nurturing emotional connections demand consistent effort. Vulnerability, honest communication, and understanding transform relationships and lead to the joy and fulfilment they seek. Walls built by instability can be replaced with bridges of connection and trust.

Mental instability stagnates personal growth. Healing, though daunting, is essential. Progress begins with accountability, self-awareness, and seeking help. Breaking cycles of suffering for oneself and others paves the way for a purposeful and peaceful life. The journey requires strength, compassion, and boundaries, both for individuals and those supporting them. Empathy should not come at the cost of one's mental health. Together, healing becomes possible, creating a legacy of resilience and connection.

XXI

15. Emotions as a Gateway to Spiritual Growth

Emotions as the Gateway

Emotions are the essence of human experience, deeply influencing our inner and outer worlds. Beyond their role in shaping thoughts and actions, emotions serve as a profound gateway to spiritual health. They connect us to our higher selves, guide our understanding of life's deeper meanings, and foster a sense of unity with the universe. By embracing and understanding our emotions, we can embark on a journey of spiritual awakening and holistic well-being.

The Link Between Emotions and Spirituality

Spiritual health refers to a sense of purpose, inner peace, and connection to something greater than oneself be it a higher power, nature, or the collective human spirit. Emotions act as bridges between the material and spiritual realms, grounding abstract spiritual concepts in human experience.

Positive emotions like love, gratitude, and compassion elevate the spirit, encouraging feelings of interconnectedness and transcendence. These emotions foster a state of flow, where the boundaries of self dissolve, allowing us to connect with the divine or the universal energy. On the other hand, even challenging emotions like grief, anger, or fear can serve as spiritual teachers, pushing us to seek meaning, growth, and healing.

Emotions as Catalysts for Spiritual Growth

1. Gratitude and Joy: Gratitude opens the heart and mind to the abundance of life, fostering an appreciation for both the ordinary and the extraordinary. Similarly, joy uplifts the spirit, creating a direct line to the sacred. These emotions nurture spiritual health by promoting a sense of fulfilment and connection.

2. Love and Compassion: Love transcends the personal, inspiring acts of kindness and altruism that enrich the soul. Compassion, a deeper understanding of others' suffering, connects us to the shared human experience, fostering a profound spiritual bond.

3. Sorrow and Grief: While often seen as negative, emotions like sorrow and grief can be transformative. They force introspection, inviting us to confront life's impermanence and seek solace in spirituality. Many spiritual practices, from meditation to prayer, emerge as tools to navigate these emotional landscapes.

4. Anger and Frustration: These emotions, when channelled constructively, can inspire change and personal growth. They reveal unmet needs or imbalances, pushing us toward deeper self-awareness and alignment with our spiritual values.

The Role of Emotional Awareness in Spiritual Health

Emotional awareness is essential for spiritual growth. By observing and understanding emotions without judgment, we can uncover their deeper significance. Practices like mindfulness and meditation allow us to sit with our emotions, gaining insight into the thoughts and beliefs that drive them.

For instance, the practice of loving-kindness meditation involves cultivating feelings of compassion and goodwill toward oneself and others. This simple act of focusing on positive emotions can shift our spiritual state, enhancing inner peace and connectedness.

Emotions and the Energy Body

Many spiritual traditions view emotions as energetic forces that influence the body and mind. In systems like Ayurveda or Traditional Chinese Medicine, emotions are believed to flow through energy centers or meridians, affecting physical and spiritual health. Practices such as yoga, Reiki, or breathwork help balance these energies, creating harmony and fostering spiritual well-being.

For example, feelings of fear are often associated with the root chakra, which governs our sense of security and grounding. Addressing this fear through spiritual practices can restore balance, enabling personal and spiritual growth.

Emotional Intelligence as a Spiritual Tool

Emotional intelligence (EI) is the ability to recognize, understand, and manage emotions plays a crucial role in spiritual health. High EI allows individuals to process emotions constructively, fostering forgiveness, empathy, and inner peace. These qualities are integral to many spiritual traditions, which emphasize virtues like humility, compassion, and self-awareness.

Cultivating Spiritual Health Through Emotions

To harness emotions as a gateway to spiritual health, consider the following practices:

1. Mindful Reflection: Take time to observe your emotions without judgment. Journaling or meditating on emotional experiences can provide clarity and insight into your spiritual journey.

2. Practice Gratitude: Cultivate a daily habit of acknowledging the blessings in your life. Gratitude amplifies spiritual awareness and fosters a sense of abundance.

3. Embrace Forgiveness: Release resentment and anger by practicing forgiveness. This liberates emotional energy and aligns you with higher spiritual states.

4. Connect with Nature: Spending time in nature can evoke feelings of awe and interconnectedness, nurturing both emotional and spiritual health.

5. Engage in Rituals or Prayer: These practices channel emotions into meaningful expressions, deepening your spiritual connection.

Emotions are not just fleeting states of mind; they are profound messengers that connect us to the spiritual dimensions of life. By understanding and embracing the full spectrum of our emotions, we unlock the potential for deeper self-awareness, inner peace, and transcendence. Emotions are the compass guiding us through the complexities of human experience toward spiritual enlightenment. They remind us that every feeling joyful or painful is a step on the path to wholeness and harmony.

ॐ

Love and Humanity: The Path to a Fulfilled Life

Love and humanity are the cornerstones of a meaningful existence. They go beyond fleeting emotions, serving as a guiding force that connects us with others and helps us discover our deeper purpose. To love selflessly is to extend compassion, understanding, and care to those around us, not for recognition but for the sheer joy of uplifting another soul.

When we embrace humanity, empathy, generosity, and kindness; we recognize the interwoven fabric of life where every action, no matter how small, creates ripples of positivity. By contributing to the happiness of others, we transcend personal struggles and experience the profound satisfaction of knowing we've made a difference. This outward focus, paradoxically, nourishes our inner growth and sense of fulfilment.

Living a purpose-driven life means aligning our talents and resources with the betterment of the world around us. It's in the moments of selfless giving, whether through a kind word, a helping hand, or a shared smile, that we find true happiness and peace. Love and humanity are not just values; they are the ultimate legacy we leave behind, reminding us that our purpose lies not in what we gain, but in what we give.

When we choose to live with love and humanity, we unlock the potential for profound personal transformation. Every act of kindness becomes a building block for a world that thrives on mutual respect and care. This doesn't require grand gestures; often, it is the simplest acts of listening without judgment, supporting someone in need, or sharing a moment of joy that create a lasting impact.

As we give of ourselves, we learn an invaluable truth, happiness multiplies when shared. The love we pour into the lives of others returns to us in unexpected and beautiful ways, enriching our own journey. It is through these connections that we begin to understand the essence of our existence that our lives are not separate, but intricately linked with the lives of others.

This realization brings a sense of completeness. When we see our actions light up someone else's life, we are reminded of our own power to heal, inspire, and nurture. Our purpose unfolds in these moments of giving and connecting, filling the voids in our own hearts with the joy of being part of something greater than ourselves.

Ultimately, to love and serve humanity is to honour the shared essence that makes us human. It is a journey of continual learning, where every step taken in love leads to deeper fulfilment. By living with intention, rooted in empathy and care, we not only shape a better world but also discover the profound satisfaction of a life well-lived. This is the heart of purpose to leave the world brighter, to touch lives with kindness, and to know that our presence has made a meaningful difference.

Likewise, we make circles for ourselves in the sense of caste religion race something to differentiate from self to others which brings a lot of hatred and provokes anger in someone because they are not us, they are differentiated by different religions or something how these kill humanity in us.

The barriers we create whether based on caste, religion, race, or any other form of identity serve as invisible walls that divide us from the shared essence of humanity. These divisions, though often rooted in tradition or societal constructs, are powerful tools of separation that perpetuate misunderstanding, prejudice, and conflict. When we define ourselves solely by these labels, we lose sight of the common thread that binds us all as human beings.

By focusing on these differences, we unintentionally foster an "us versus them" mentality, which breeds fear, anger, and resentment. Instead of seeing another person as an individual with hopes, struggles, and dreams, we reduce them to a label or stereotype. This reduction dehumanizes, erases empathy, and creates a fertile ground for hatred and violence. The walls we build in our minds eventually manifest in the world around us, stifling love and extinguishing the light of humanity.

This process doesn't just harm others; it also kills something vital within us. Our ability to empathize diminishes, our capacity for connection weakens, and the natural human inclination to love and cooperate is suppressed. Over time, the divisions we uphold isolate us from the richness of diversity and the joy of understanding perspectives beyond our own.

To heal this, we must begin by recognizing the illusion of separateness. At our core, we are more alike than we are different our laughter, tears, and aspirations echo the same humanity.

Breaking free from these mental and societal constructs requires courage and self-awareness. It means choosing love over fear, curiosity over judgment, and unity over division.

When we actively seek to understand and embrace those who are different from us, we rediscover the boundless potential of humanity. We learn that diversity is not a threat but a gift, offering endless opportunities to grow, connect, and create together. By dissolving these barriers, we don't just restore humanity in others; we also restore it in ourselves. In doing so, we reclaim our ability to love fully and to build a world where kindness and compassion know no boundaries.

As we dismantle these barriers, we begin to see how our differences whether in culture, beliefs, or traditions are not obstacles but expressions of the infinite ways humanity manifests. Each person's story adds depth to the collective human experience, and our ability to embrace this diversity reflects the strength of our character.

When we choose to define ourselves by what unites us rather than what divides us, we open the door to deeper understanding. Love and empathy flourish when we approach others with humility, recognizing that no single perspective holds the entirety of truth. This shift in mindset transforms encounters into opportunities for learning, connection, and growth.

However, overcoming these deeply ingrained divisions requires effort. It means confronting our biases, unlearning prejudices, and resisting the societal norms that perpetuate division. It means choosing to have uncomfortable conversations, stepping out of echo chambers, and refusing to be complicit in systems that dehumanize others. This process can be challenging, but it is necessary for cultivating true humanity within us.

When we stop seeing others through the lens of caste, religion, race, or other divisive identities, we begin to see them simply as people complex, flawed, and beautiful, just like us. This recognition rekindles the humanity within us, reminding us that love and compassion are not limited resources. They expand infinitely when shared.

By breaking free from these self-imposed circles, we can collectively create a world where our shared humanity takes precedence over our differences. It's a world where kindness is not conditional, respect is universal, and love is the bridge that connects us all. In this world, we find not only the essence of humanity but also the true fulfilment of our purpose: to leave a legacy of understanding, harmony, and compassion for generations to come.

When we let go of the "othering" mindset, we reclaim our innate ability to love unconditionally. We transform ourselves and the world around us, nurturing a humanity that thrives on inclusion and care. In this unity lies the path to healing, growth, and the collective fulfilment of a shared purpose building a life, and a world, where everyone belongs.

How agony and hatred affect our mental health and happiness

Agony and hurt, when left unresolved, can deeply impact our mental health and overall happiness. Emotional pain whether caused by betrayal, loss, rejection, or trauma creates a ripple effect in our minds and bodies, influencing how we think, feel, and interact with the world around us.

1. The Mental Health Impact

Emotional Turmoil: Prolonged feelings of hurt can lead to persistent sadness, anger, or frustration. This emotional turbulence often clouds our ability to process situations rationally and affects our daily decision-making.

Stress and Anxiety: Painful experiences activate our body's stress response, flooding us with cortisol and other stress hormones. Over time, this can lead to chronic anxiety, worry, or a heightened sense of fear and insecurity.

Depression: Deep hurt can contribute to feelings of hopelessness and isolation, which are key markers of depression. When emotional pain lingers, it can erode our self-worth and make us feel disconnected from life's joys.

Negative Thought Patterns: Hurt often gives rise to self-critical or pessimistic thinking. We might replay painful memories, blame ourselves, or develop a fear of vulnerability, all of which perpetuate mental distress.

2. Effects on Happiness

Loss of Joy: When consumed by pain, it becomes difficult to appreciate positive experiences. Even moments of happiness may feel fleeting or overshadowed by the weight of unresolved emotions.

Damaged Relationships: Hurt can strain relationships, as unresolved emotions might lead to mistrust, resentment, or withdrawal. This isolation further diminishes happiness, as humans thrive on meaningful connections.

Lack of Purpose: Prolonged emotional distress can make life feel directionless. It becomes challenging to focus on personal goals, passions, or a sense of purpose when pain dominates the mental landscape.

3. Physical Manifestations

Emotional hurt doesn't just affect the mind, it often manifests physically. Headaches, fatigue, digestive issues, or weakened immunity can all stem from unprocessed pain, creating a cycle where mental and physical health deteriorate together.

4. Breaking the Cycle

The key to healing lies in acknowledging and addressing the hurt, rather than suppressing it. Strategies to reclaim mental health and happiness include:

Acceptance: Recognize your pain without judgment. It's valid to feel hurt, but it doesn't define your worth or future.

Seeking Support: Sharing your feelings with trusted friends, family, or a therapist can help process the pain and reduce its burden.

Practicing Self-Compassion: Treat yourself with kindness and patience. Allow yourself the space to heal without rushing the process.

Mindfulness and Reflection: Practices like meditation or journaling can help bring clarity and reduce emotional reactivity, allowing you to observe your thoughts without becoming overwhelmed.

Channelling Hurt into Growth: Pain often carries lessons. Reflecting on what you can learn or how you can grow from the experience can be transformative.

While agony and hurt are inevitable parts of life, they don't have to define our mental state or happiness. Healing is a journey that requires time, effort, and support, but it ultimately leads to resilience, self-awareness, and the ability to find joy even after hardship.

5. The Power of Letting Go

One of the most transformative steps in overcoming agony and hurt is learning to let go. This doesn't mean dismissing or forgetting the pain, it means releasing its hold over you. Holding on to anger, resentment, or grief keeps you tethered to the source of your suffering, preventing you from moving forward. 'Letting go' is an act of self-liberation, a choice to prioritize your peace over the weight of past hurts.

Forgiveness: Forgiving others (or even yourself) is not about excusing the wrongdoing but about freeing yourself from the emotional chains of bitterness. Forgiveness allows you to reclaim your power and focus on the present rather than being stuck in the past.

Reframing Experiences: Sometimes, shifting your perspective can lessen the sting of hurt. Instead of seeing it solely as a source of pain, view it as an opportunity for growth or a stepping stone toward resilience.

Acceptance of Imperfection: Recognizing that life and people are imperfect helps in managing expectations. Understanding that hurt is a natural part of human interactions can reduce feelings of betrayal or disappointment.

6. Rebuilding Mental Health and Happiness

Once you begin addressing the root causes of your pain, it's important to actively rebuild your mental health and cultivate happiness. Here's how:

Nurture Positive Relationships: Surround yourself with people who uplift and support you. Building trust and intimacy with others helps to heal the emotional wounds caused by hurt.

Practice Gratitude: Focusing on the good things in your life, even small ones, can shift your mindset and create a foundation for happiness. Gratitude helps counterbalance negative emotions.

Engage in Purposeful Activities: Pursuing hobbies, volunteering, or working toward personal goals gives your life direction and fulfilment, helping you focus beyond the pain.

Prioritize Self-Care: Exercise, eat healthily, get enough sleep, and engage in activities that bring you joy. Physical well-being is closely tied to mental health.

Develop Emotional Resilience: Strengthen your ability to cope with adversity by practicing mindfulness, maintaining a positive outlook, and seeking support when needed.

7. Finding Meaning in the Pain

Sometimes, the most painful experiences carry within them the seeds of profound transformation. Reflecting on what the hurt has taught you whether it's patience, empathy, or the importance of boundaries can bring clarity and purpose. Many find that their pain inspires them to help others, turning their struggles into a source of strength for themselves and their communities.

8. Choosing Happiness as a Path

Happiness is not the absence of pain but the ability to navigate through it while finding joy and meaning in life. By addressing hurt and taking intentional steps to heal, you reclaim control over your mental and emotional well-being. You learn that while pain may shape you, it doesn't have to define you.

In the end, agony and hurt are reminders of our humanity. They show us our capacity to feel deeply and connect with others. By facing these emotions head-on and embracing the lessons they bring, we not only heal but also grow into more compassionate, resilient, and fulfilled individuals. Happiness becomes not just an outcome but a way of living, anchored in love, self-awareness, and the strength to rise above life's inevitable challenges.

XXII

16. The Holistic Feedback Loop: A Balanced System

The Holistic Feedback Loop: A Balanced System

The concept of the holistic feedback loop lies at the heart of understanding how interconnected systems of mind, body, emotions, and spirit work together to create a balanced and thriving human experience. This loop illustrates the dynamic interplay between these dimensions, showing how changes in one area ripple through the others, shaping overall well-being.

When all elements of this system are in harmony, they reinforce each other positively, creating a feedback loop that supports health, happiness, and fulfilment. Conversely, imbalances in one domain can disrupt the entire system, underscoring the need for an integrated approach to wellness.

The Components of the Holistic Feedback Loop

1. The Physical Body

The physical body is the most tangible aspect of the system. It serves as the foundation for energy, mobility, and vitality. Nutrition, exercise, sleep, and medical care are essential inputs that determine physical health. When the body is strong and resilient, it supports mental clarity, emotional stability, and spiritual awareness. Conversely, physical ailments or neglect can disrupt the entire feedback loop, manifesting as fatigue, stress, or emotional imbalance.

2. The Mind

The mind governs thoughts, beliefs, and cognitive processes. It interprets the world and determines how we respond to challenges and opportunities. Positive thought patterns and mental resilience enhance problem-solving abilities and emotional regulation. However, chronic stress, negative thinking, or mental overload can derail the loop, affecting the body through hormonal imbalances and impacting emotional health.

3. Emotions

Emotions are the bridge between the mind and the spirit. They provide immediate feedback on our experiences, guiding our decisions and interactions. Positive emotions like joy, love, and gratitude enhance the loop by fostering mental and physical health, while negative emotions like anger or fear, when unresolved, can lead to stress, inflammation, and disconnection.

4. The Spirit

The spirit represents a sense of purpose, inner peace, and connection to a higher power or the universe. Spiritual health aligns the system, offering clarity and meaning that can inspire healthier choices and balanced emotions. Disconnection from spiritual practices or a sense of purpose can disrupt the loop, often manifesting as feelings of emptiness or stagnation.

How the Feedback Loop Operates

The holistic feedback loop operates through dynamic interactions between these components:

Mind to Body: Positive mental health fosters physical well-being through healthy behaviours, reduced stress, and improved immunity. For example, a person with a resilient mindset is more likely to engage in regular exercise or maintain a balanced diet.

Body to Mind: A healthy body supports mental clarity and emotional resilience. Regular physical activity, for instance, increases endorphin levels, reducing anxiety and enhancing cognitive function.

Emotions to Spirit: Positive emotions like gratitude and compassion deepen spiritual connection, creating a sense of purpose and harmony. This, in turn, strengthens emotional stability and fosters resilience.

Spirit to Emotions: A strong spiritual foundation provides perspective and inner peace, enabling the regulation of emotions and reducing the impact of stress or fear.

Imbalances and Disruptions

When one aspect of the loop is disrupted, the effects can cascade through the system:

Chronic Stress: Prolonged stress can overstimulate the mind, leading to physical symptoms like fatigue, hormonal imbalances, and weakened immunity. It can also create emotional instability, further straining the system.

Poor Physical Health: Illness or neglect of the body can cloud the mind, intensify negative emotions, and diminish spiritual connection, creating a downward spiral.

Emotional Suppression: Ignoring or repressing emotions can lead to unresolved conflicts that strain mental health and manifest as physical ailments like tension headaches or digestive issues.

Lack of Spiritual Fulfilment: Disconnection from purpose or spiritual practices can result in feelings of emptiness, which can amplify stress and emotional instability, affecting physical health.

Restoring Balance in the Feedback Loop

Restoring balance requires a holistic approach that addresses all aspects of the system:

1. Physical Care: Prioritize exercise, balanced nutrition, and restorative sleep to support the body's resilience and energy.

2. Mental Health: Practice mindfulness, journaling, or cognitive behavioural techniques to foster positive thinking and mental clarity.

3. Emotional Awareness: Embrace emotions as valuable feedback, processing them through healthy outlets like communication, art, or therapy.

4. Spiritual Connection: Engage in practices like meditation, prayer, or spending time in nature to cultivate inner peace and purpose.

The Synergy of the Balanced System

When the feedback loop is in harmony, the system operates synergistically, amplifying well-being in all areas. A healthy body fuels a sharp mind; a sharp mind nurtures positive emotions; positive emotions deepen spiritual connections, which in turn inspire actions that sustain the body. This virtuous cycle creates a self-reinforcing system of health, happiness, and fulfilment.

The holistic feedback loop is a dynamic and interconnected system that underscores the importance of addressing the whole person's body, mind, emotions, and spirit. By recognizing the interplay between these dimensions and striving for balance, individuals can achieve a state of harmony that supports long-term health and well-being. Embracing this integrated approach empowers us to not only heal but to thrive, cultivating a life of purpose, connection, and vitality.

Spiritual Health: A Holistic Perspective

Spiritual health is the essence of aligning oneself with the universe and understanding the deeper purpose of existence. It transcends religious beliefs, rituals, or the worship of specific deities. Instead, it emphasizes the interconnectedness of all life forms and the energies that bind the universe together.

The Universe and Spirituality

The universe is a vast system of energies and elements. Our bodies, made from the five elements of earth, water, fire, air, and space are direct manifestations of this universal energy. The food we consume grows from the soil, transforming into our physical selves. This cycle reflects our unity with nature and the cosmos. Recognizing this interconnectedness helps us understand that we are both contributors to and beneficiaries of the universal ecosystem.

The Role of Consciousness

Achieving spiritual health begins with reaching a heightened state of consciousness. This involves deep self-awareness and understanding our place within the greater scheme of the universe.

When we align with this consciousness. We perceive the universe's purpose. We recognize our role, whether small or large, in contributing positively to other beings. We find meaning and fulfilment in our actions, regardless of their scale.

God and Belief Systems

God, in this context, is a human creation meant to simplify complex spiritual concepts. Gods act as symbols or resources to help channel energy and focus. When beliefs in gods serve to inspire, uplift, and guide individuals toward positivity and higher purpose, they are beneficial. However, when these beliefs cause conflict, division, or degrade humanity by fostering negativity, they lose their spiritual essence. Spirituality is not about imposing beliefs but enhancing humanity. True spiritual health promotes peace, compassion, and respect for others, irrespective of caste, religion, or cultural differences.

The Path to Spiritual Health

Spiritual health requires a journey from the physical to the metaphysical:

1. Acceptance and Self-Awareness: Accept who you are and strive to understand yourself better. Acknowledge your strengths, weaknesses, and the reality of your existence.

2. Connecting with Purpose: Identify a higher purpose in life, which could range from personal growth to contributing meaningfully to society or the environment.

3. Living in Harmony: Align your actions with the principles of nature and universal balance. Going against this harmony leads to chaos and disaster.

4. Transformation and Contribution: Serve others with love, compassion, and humanity. True spiritual health involves selfless acts that enhance the lives of others and the environment.

5. Reaching Higher Consciousness: Progress from fulfilling basic needs to understanding your soul and spirit. Challenges from the universe are opportunities to grow and connect with higher consciousness.

The Essence of Spiritual Health

Spiritual health is about living a life of balance, purpose, and contribution. It is acceptance of reality which is understanding yourself and the universe without clinging to assumptions. Alignment with Nature to living in harmony with the environment and universal energies. Contribution to Humanity such as serving others, fostering peace, and uplifting those around you. Inner Peace and Enlightenment define finding satisfaction in self-awareness and spiritual growth, connecting deeply with the divine, however, you define it.

Ultimately, spiritual health is not measured by external rituals or dogmas but by your capacity to live meaningfully, love unconditionally, and contribute to the greater good of the universe. It is about transforming yourself and serving as a beacon of light for others. Continue with the description of human beings and respecting others with empathy.

The Essence of Being Human: Respect and Empathy

At the heart of spiritual health lies the essence of being human a journey defined by self-awareness, compassion, and meaningful connections. Humans, as conscious beings, are endowed with the unique ability to reflect, empathize, and act with purpose. Respect for others and empathy are cornerstones of this journey, binding us to the universal truth that all life is interconnected.

Human Beings as Part of the Universal Fabric

A human being is not an isolated entity but a vibrant thread in the fabric of the universe. Every thought, action, and interaction reverberates across the collective consciousness. To truly live as a human is to recognize the interdependence of the universe, which is to understand that every life form, from the smallest ant to the largest tree, plays a role in maintaining the balance of existence. Respect that differences in appearance, belief, or culture are expressions of the universe's infinite creativity.

Respect as a Core Value

Respect begins with acknowledging the inherent worth of every individual, irrespective of their background, choices, or circumstances. Respect yourself by valuing your uniqueness, nurturing your potential, and embracing your flaws. True self-respect fosters inner peace and strength. Respect others by recognizing their humanity, even when you disagree with them. Every person carries their struggles, dreams, and perspectives. Respect is not just tolerance it is an active appreciation of diversity and an acknowledgment of the shared essence that connects all beings.

The Role of Empathy

Empathy is the ability to step into another's shoes and feel their emotions as your own. It bridges gaps, fosters understanding, and lays the foundation for harmonious coexistence. Listen actively, without judgment, to others' stories and experiences. Open your heart to their joys, sorrows, and challenges. When people feel seen, heard, and understood, it heals wounds, dissolves conflicts, and strengthens relationships. Extend your empathy to animals, plants, and the environment. Treat every living being with kindness, as they too are part of the universal whole.

Living with Respect and Empathy

To respect and empathize with others is to contribute to a more compassionate and harmonious world. It requires suspending judgment to let go of biases and preconceived notions. Approach people and situations with an open mind. Understand that everyone's journey is different. Patience allows space for growth and understanding. Lift people instead of tearing them down. Celebrate their successes and support them through their struggles.

Empathy and Spiritual Growth

Empathy is the path to higher consciousness. When you care for others selflessly, you transcend the ego and align with the universe's purpose. Respecting others and feeling their pain and joy as your own is a spiritual act; it connects your soul to the greater collective and deepens your sense of purpose.

The Ripple Effect of Empathy

Acts of empathy and respect create ripples of positivity within families. They foster love, trust, and understanding. They break barriers, resolve conflicts, and encourage cooperation within communities. They inspire movements for equality, justice, and environmental stewardship globally which is all we need to aspire.

Respecting and Empathizing with Yourself

True respect and empathy begin with the self. When you acknowledge your feelings and accept your emotions without suppressing or denying them. Forgive Yourself and understand that mistakes are part of growth. Learn from them instead of dwelling in guilt. Care for yourself by prioritizing your physical, mental, and spiritual well-being. This inner harmony allows you to extend the same understanding to others, creating a cycle of mutual respect and compassion.

A Human Being in Harmony

To live as a spiritually aligned human being is to embrace respect and empathy as guiding principles. It is to see the universe in every living being and to act with love and understanding. By doing so, we elevate ourselves and contribute to the collective growth of humanity, creating a world where everyone and everything thrives in unity. More about love for others and how we should love others without judging to see ourselves in their shoes.

XXIII

Checklists and Self-Assessments

Here's a checklist and self-assessment guide that focuses on love, boundaries, and relationships. This will help you reflect on your current relationship dynamics, your own needs, and areas for personal growth:

Checklist for Healthy Boundaries in Relationships:

Clear Communication:

- Do I express my needs and desires openly and honestly?
- Do I feel comfortable speaking up when something doesn't feel right or when I'm uncomfortable?

Respect for Space:

- Do I honour my own need for personal time and space, and do I respect others' need for space as well?
- Am I aware of when I need alone time and able to communicate that to my partner or loved ones?

Mutual Respect:

- Do I respect others' opinions, values, and feelings even when they differ from my own?
- Do I expect respect in return and address situations where disrespect occurs?

Emotional Boundaries:

- Do I take responsibility for my own emotions, or do I allow others to make me feel responsible for theirs?
- Can I express my emotions in a way that is healthy and constructive?

Physical Boundaries:

- Do I feel comfortable with the level of physical affection or intimacy in my relationships?

- ○ Do I communicate my physical boundaries clearly, and do others respect them?

Time and Energy:

- ○ Am I able to say "no" without feeling guilty when I am overwhelmed or need time for myself?
- ○ Do I prioritize my time and energy to focus on people and activities that nourish me?

Reciprocity:

- ○ Do I feel that my efforts are reciprocated in my relationships, whether emotionally, physically, or mentally?
- ○ Am I being appreciated for my contributions, and am I also acknowledging others' efforts?

Self-Assessment for Personal Growth and Relationship Health:

Self-Worth and Relationships:

- Do I value myself independently of how others treat me? (Yes/No)
- How often do I find myself seeking external validation in my relationships? (Rarely/Sometimes/Frequently)

- Am I comfortable with my own company and needs, or do I rely on others to fulfill my sense of self-worth? (Comfortable/Somewhat Comfortable/Not Comfortable)

Emotional Health and Awareness:

- When faced with conflict, do I approach the situation calmly and constructively? (Yes/No)
- How well do I recognize and manage my emotions in relationships? (Well/Moderately/Needs Improvement)
- Do I take time to process my feelings before reacting to others? (Yes/No)

Boundaries in Relationships:

- Do I have clear boundaries in my romantic, family, and friendship relationships? (Yes/No)
- Am I able to maintain my boundaries without feeling guilty? (Yes/No)
- Have I allowed my boundaries to be crossed in the past? (Yes/No) If yes, how can I handle such situations differently in the future?

Trust and Vulnerability:

- Do I trust others easily, or do I tend to be cautious and guarded? (Easily/Cautiously/Not Easily)
- How vulnerable do I allow myself to be with those closest to me? (Very Vulnerable/Somewhat Vulnerable/Not Vulnerable)

- Do I feel safe to express my true self in my relationships? (Yes/No)

Love and Communication:

- Do I openly communicate my feelings, needs, and expectations in my relationships? (Yes/No)
- How well do I listen and empathize with my partner/friends/family when they share their feelings? (Very Well/Moderately/Needs Improvement)
- Do I regularly check in with my loved ones about their emotional needs? (Yes/No)

Patterns and Growth in Relationships:

- Can I identify any recurring patterns in my relationships (e.g., attracting toxic people, becoming overly dependent)? (Yes/No)
- What are the main lessons I've learned from past relationships, and how have they shaped my approach to current relationships?
- How open am I to personal growth and change in the context of my relationships? (Very Open/Somewhat Open/Not Open)

Love Languages and Needs:

- Do I know my love language, and can I communicate it to others? (Yes/No)
- Can I identify my partner's/loved ones' love languages? (Yes/No)

- How often do I feel that my emotional needs are being met in my relationships? (Always/Sometimes/Rarely)

Conflict Resolution:

- How do I typically react during conflict? (Calmly/Defensively/Angrily)
- Am I able to forgive and move on after conflicts, or do I hold grudges? (Yes/No)
- Do I approach conflict with the goal of resolution, or do I tend to avoid it? (Resolution/Avoidance)

Forgiveness and Healing:

- Is there anyone I need to forgive in order to move forward in my personal healing? (Yes/No)
- How do I practice forgiveness, both for myself and others? (Regularly/Sometimes/Hardly Ever)

Reflection on Your Self-Assessment:

After completing the checklist and self-assessment, take time to reflect on the following:

1. **What stood out to you the most during this exercise?**
2. **Which areas do you feel confident in, and which areas need attention?**
3. **What changes or improvements would you like to make to build healthier relationships?**

4. **How can you better honour your boundaries and your emotional needs in relationships moving forward?**

This checklist and self-assessment provide a structured way to reflect on your relationships, boundaries, and emotional well-being. Regular reflection like this can guide you toward healthier, more fulfilling connections with yourself and others.

Here's a **self-assessment** focusing on **mental, emotional, and spiritual well-being**. This guide helps you reflect on different aspects of your well-being and identify areas for growth and improvement.

Mental Well-Being:

Mental Clarity:

- Do I feel mentally clear and focused on my daily life? (Yes/No)
- How often do I feel overwhelmed by my thoughts or the demands of life? (Rarely/Sometimes/Often)
- Do I regularly practice techniques to calm my mind, such as meditation or mindfulness? (Yes/No)

Stress Management:

- How effectively do I handle stress? (Very Well/Moderately/Not Well)
- When I experience stress, do I have healthy coping strategies, such as exercising, talking it out, or journaling? (Yes/No)

- Do I recognize the early signs of stress and take action to manage it? (Yes/No)

Mental Growth:

- Do I actively seek to learn and grow mentally, such as reading, studying, or engaging in new experiences? (Yes/No)
- How often do I challenge my thinking and beliefs to expand my understanding? (Regularly/Sometimes/Rarely)

Focus and Productivity:

- Am I able to maintain focus on tasks without getting easily distracted? (Yes/No)
- Do I feel productive and efficient in managing my responsibilities? (Yes/No)
- Do I set clear goals and take actionable steps to achieve them? (Yes/No)

Emotional Well-Being:

Self-Awareness:

- Am I in touch with my emotions and able to identify how I'm feeling in the moment? (Yes/No)

- Do I allow myself to feel and express my emotions rather than suppress them? (Yes/No)
- How often do I check in with myself to understand my emotional state? (Regularly/Sometimes/Rarely)

Emotional Regulation:

- Do I manage my emotions in a healthy way, without letting them control me? (Yes/No)
- When I feel upset or angry, am I able to calm myself down before reacting? (Yes/No)
- Do I avoid emotional outbursts or letting my emotions negatively affect others? (Yes/No)

Resilience and Coping:

- How well do I bounce back from difficult or challenging situations? (Very Well/Moderately/Not Well)
- Do I have a support system of people I can rely on when facing emotional struggles? (Yes/No)
- Am I able to learn and grow from difficult emotional experiences? (Yes/No)

Self-Compassion:

- How often do I practice self-compassion and speak kindly to myself? (Regularly/Sometimes/Rarely)
- When I make mistakes, do I treat myself with understanding and forgiveness? (Yes/No)

- ○ Do I acknowledge my accomplishments and strengths, or am I quick to dismiss them? (Yes/No)

Spiritual Well-Being:

Sense of Purpose:

- ○ Do I feel a sense of purpose and direction in my life? (Yes/No)
- ○ How clear am I about my values, and do I live in alignment with them? (Very Clear/Somewhat Clear/Not Clear)
- ○ Do I regularly reflect on my life's purpose and what gives me meaning? (Yes/No)

Connection to Something Greater:

- ○ Do I feel connected to something greater than myself, whether that's a higher power, nature, or a sense of community? (Yes/No)
- ○ How often do I engage in spiritual or contemplative practices, such as prayer, meditation, or mindfulness? (Regularly/ Sometimes/Rarely)
- ○ Do I feel a sense of inner peace and tranquility from my spiritual practices? (Yes/No)

Gratitude and Contentment:

- ○ Do I regularly practice gratitude and focus on the positive aspects of my life? (Yes/No)

- ○ How often do I find myself feeling content and at peace with what I have in life? (Always/Sometimes/Rarely)
- ○ Do I feel a sense of connection and appreciation for the present moment? (Yes/No)

Growth and Transformation:

- ○ Do I embrace personal growth and transformation as part of my spiritual journey? (Yes/No)
- ○ How open am I to exploring new spiritual ideas, practices, and perspectives? (Very Open/Somewhat Open/Not Open)
- ○ Do I find meaning in overcoming challenges, seeing them as opportunities for spiritual growth? (Yes/No)

Self-Reflection on Mental, Emotional, and Spiritual Well-Being:

After completing this self-assessment, reflect on the following:

1. **What areas of mental, emotional, and spiritual well-being feel strong to me?**
2. **Where do I feel there is room for growth or improvement in these areas?**
3. **What specific actions or practices could I incorporate into my life to improve my mental, emotional, and spiritual health?**
4. **What is one small step I can take today to enhance my well-being in one of these areas?**

By assessing these key areas, you can gain greater awareness of your current state of well-being and create a plan for further growth and improvement in your mental, emotional, and spiritual health.

XXIV
Reflection Prompts

Awareness and Self-discovery prompts

Here are some reflection prompts focused on awareness and self-discovery:

Core Values

"What are the three values that guide your decisions and actions? How do these values shape the way you interact with others and approach challenges in your life?"

Personal Strengths and Weaknesses

"Reflect on your strengths and weaknesses. How do these qualities influence your personal growth? What are you doing to build on your strengths, and how are you working on your weaknesses?"

Life Purpose

"What do you feel your life's purpose or mission is at this moment? How do your current actions and choices align with this sense of purpose?"

Emotional Awareness

"How do you typically respond to stressful situations or emotional challenges? What patterns can you identify in your reactions, and how can you work toward healthier responses?"

Self-Compassion

"Think about a time when you were hard on yourself. What would you say to a friend in the same situation? How can you practice more self-compassion in your everyday life?"

Self-Limiting Beliefs

"What beliefs or thought patterns hold you back from reaching your full potential? How can you challenge these beliefs to create more room for growth and change?"

Passions and Interests

"What activities or hobbies make you feel most alive and connected to yourself? How often do you make time for these activities, and how can you incorporate them more into your daily life?"

Personal Growth

"In what ways have you grown over the past year? What lessons have you learned, and how have they shaped your sense of self?"

Self-Expression

"How do you express your true self to others? Are there areas in your life where you feel you're holding back? What can you do to be more authentic in your interactions?"

Inner Peace and Fulfilment

"When do you feel most at peace with yourself? What are the circumstances or habits that allow you to feel fulfilled, and how can you cultivate more of these moments?"

These reflection prompts can help deepen your understanding of yourself, uncover your true desires, and guide your journey toward personal growth and fulfilment.

Love, Boundaries, and Relationships

Here are some reflection prompts focused on love, boundaries, and relationships to help with self-discovery and awareness:

Understanding Love

"What does love mean to you? How do you express love, and how do you feel most loved by others? How have your experiences with love shaped your relationships today?"

Healthy Boundaries

"What does having healthy boundaries look like for you in relationships? Are there any areas in your life where you struggle to set or maintain boundaries, and what could you do to improve this?"

Respect and Reciprocity

"In your closest relationships, do you feel there is mutual respect and reciprocity? How do you ensure that your needs are being met while also meeting the needs of others?"

Conflict Resolution

"How do you typically handle conflict in relationships? Do you find it difficult to express your feelings or stand up for yourself? How can you approach conflicts more healthily and constructively?"

Self-Worth and Relationships

"How do you perceive your own self-worth in the context of your relationships? Do you often find your value reflected in how others treat you, or do you maintain your sense of self-worth independently?"

Love and Independence

"How do you balance your own independence with being in a loving relationship? Do you feel that your individuality is respected and nurtured, or do you struggle with co-dependency?"

Boundaries with Family

"What are the boundaries you've set with family members, and how do they impact your well-being? Are there any family dynamics that you feel need to change to improve your relationships?"

Attraction vs. Attachment

"What qualities do you find yourself attracted to in others? How often does your attraction come from genuine connection versus attachment or dependency on others?"

Love Languages

"What is your love language, and how does it influence the way you give and receive love in your relationships? How can you communicate your needs better to those who are important to you?"

Forgiveness and Healing

"Think about a past relationship where there was hurt or disappointment. Have you fully forgiven both yourself and the other person? What would forgiveness look like in this situation, and how could it help you heal?"

Trust and Vulnerability

"How easy or difficult is it for you to trust others in relationships? What fears or past experiences might be holding you back from being more vulnerable with those you love?"

Relationship Patterns

"Reflect on the patterns in your past relationships. Are there recurring themes or behaviors that you notice in yourself or others? How can you break these patterns to build healthier, more fulfilling relationships?"

Letting Go of Toxic Relationships

"Are there any relationships in your life that feel draining or toxic? How do you differentiate between a relationship that requires healing and one that may need to be let go of for your well-being?"

Supporting Your Partner's Growth

"In your romantic relationships, how do you support your partner's growth and independence? How do you ensure that both of you continue to grow individually while also nurturing the bond between you?"

Setting Boundaries with Intimacy

"How do you set boundaries in intimate relationships? Are there any emotional or physical boundaries you feel are being crossed, and how can you communicate them effectively?"

These prompts can deepen your understanding of how you navigate love, set boundaries, and maintain healthy, fulfilling relationships. Reflecting on these areas can guide you toward more meaningful connections and personal growth.

XXV

Closing with a Vision for Readers

The Concept of God: A Universal Perspective

The idea of God, as you describe, transcends religious boundaries, rituals, and regional identities. It is not about idols or specific practices but a higher consciousness and the universal energy that governs existence. This perspective allows for a deeper, more inclusive understanding of God as the source of creation, the force of nature, and the essence of life itself.

God as the Universal Energy

A Source of Life: God is the creative force that brings life into being, encompassing the five elements such as earth, water, fire, air, and space. These elements form the foundation of all living beings, connecting us to the cosmos.

An Infinite Consciousness: God is not a singular entity but the collective consciousness of the universe. It represents harmony, balance, and purpose.

A Reflection of Nature: The cycles of birth, growth, decay, and renewal in nature are manifestations of this divine energy. God is evident in the beauty of a blooming flower, the strength of a mountain, and the rhythm of the oceans.

God as a Human Creation for Understanding

Humans created the concept of gods to simplify and relate to the abstract idea of universal energy. These representations serve as:

Resources for Guidance: Gods act as symbols or figures that inspire hope, faith, and purpose.

Ways to Channel Energy: Devotion, prayer, and rituals help focus our thoughts and intentions, aligning us with the universe's flow.

Moral Anchors: Stories and teachings associated with gods provide ethical frameworks for living harmoniously with others.

However, the value of these representations lies in their ability to uplift and unite. When the concept of God becomes a tool for division, conflict, or superiority, it loses its true essence.

The Purpose of Belief in God

Belief in God, as a universal force, serves a higher purpose:

1. Finding Peace: Connecting with God as universal energy brings inner calm and helps us align with nature's balance.

2. Seeking Light: God represents the path to enlightenment, guiding us from ignorance to understanding.

3. Fostering Humanity: True belief in God inspires love, compassion, and service to others, enhancing our connection to the world.

God and the Challenges of Life

The universe, as a manifestation of God, challenges us to grow and evolve. These challenges are not punishments but opportunities to learn and understand life's lessons through experiences, both joyful and painful. Help to transform to become better versions of ourselves by overcoming ego, fear, and negativity. It serves to use our growth which contributes positively to others and the environment. When we face challenges with faith in this higher consciousness, we align ourselves with the universe's purpose, finding strength and meaning.

God as a Guide to Spiritual Health

True belief in God should uplift the soul and guide us toward our higher purpose. This involves acceptance of reality and seeing life as it is, free from illusions and assumptions. Unity with Nature by living in harmony with the environment and respecting its cycles and rhythms. By acts of love serving others selflessly, fostering positivity, and spreading kindness.

The Misuse of God's Name:

When belief in God is used to divide based on religion, caste, or identity, justify harm or hatred, or devalue humanity, it contradicts the universal truth of love and unity. Such misuse poisons the collective spirit and creates disharmony.

A God That Connects, Not Divides

God, as the universal force, loves all beings equally, without distinction. True faith recognizes the divinity within every individual and respects their beliefs and experiences. It is the source of creation that should inspire creativity, peace, and growth, not degradation or destruction.

Living with the God You Believe In

To live aligned with this universal concept of God is to cultivate gratitude by recognizing the divine in everyday experiences, from the warmth of the sun to the kindness of others. Feel the presence of God in the interconnectedness of all life. Understand that you are part of a vast, infinite universe, yet every action of yours matters. Use your belief to inspire, heal, and uplift, creating a ripple effect of positivity.

God is a Journey, not a Destination.

God is not a being to reach but a consciousness to awaken within us. This journey involves moving from physical survival to mental clarity, from emotional balance to spiritual awakening, and ultimately aligning with the universe's higher purpose of love, creation, and harmony. By loving others, serving selflessly, and living with awareness, you connect with the God you believe in, manifesting its essence in your life and the world around you.

In the name of God how human is separated based on belief and faith in regional god and caste and community. Division in the name of God by faith, regional Gods, and social constructs lacks clarity of higher consciousness.

The concept of God was originally meant to unite, inspire, and provide a sense of purpose. However, over time, human interpretations and societal structures have led to divisions based on beliefs, regional gods, caste, and community. These separations, though rooted in cultural and historical contexts, often contradict the universal principles of love, unity, and harmony that spirituality embodies.

The Evolution of Regional Gods and Beliefs

1. Cultural Contexts:

Early humans created gods that reflected their environment, values, and challenges. For example, agricultural societies worshipped gods of rain and harvest, while warrior societies revered gods of strength and protection. Regional gods emerged as representations of local experiences, becoming central to the identity of specific communities.

2. Human Fear of the Unknown:

Belief in regional gods often provided comfort and explanations for natural phenomena or existential questions. Over time, these gods became symbols of security, leading to rigid belief systems.

3. Rituals and Customs:

Each community developed unique practices to honour their gods. These rituals became traditions, distinguishing one group from another. While these regional beliefs were initially meant to celebrate diversity, they often became tools for separation and exclusion.

Caste and Community-Based Divisions

1. The Caste System:

Originally, the caste system (e.g., varna in India) was meant to organize society based on skills and professions, ensuring balance and efficiency. Over time, it became rigid and hierarchical, associating spiritual worth and societal status with caste.

2. Exclusivity and Privilege:

Certain groups claimed superiority based on their interpretation of scriptures or their association with specific gods. This led to discrimination, marginalization, and inequality, dividing people rather than uniting them.

3. *Communal Identities:*

Communities began associating themselves with specific gods, faiths, or rituals, creating in-groups and out-groups. Faith, instead of being a personal journey, became a marker of identity, leading to division and conflict.

The Role of Power and Politics

Religious beliefs have often been manipulated for power to control the masses. Leaders and institutions used the concept of God to enforce obedience and justify societal hierarchies. Faith became a tool to mobilize communities, creating "us versus them" narratives to secure power and political divisions. Economic exploitation of rituals, pilgrimages, and religious practices were monetized, further entrenching divisions.

Faith-Based Conflicts

When beliefs in God are weaponized religion becomes exclusive instead of fostering inclusivity, faith is used to claim moral or spiritual superiority. Judgment and intolerance for differences in worship or practices lead to judgment, discrimination, and even violence. Finally leads to the erosion of humanity; core values of compassion, empathy, and unity are overshadowed by dogma and rigid interpretations.

The Consequences of Division in God's Name

1. Loss of Universal Connection: Divisions erode the sense of oneness and interconnectedness that spirituality promotes.

2. Perpetuation of Hatred: Instead of fostering love, belief systems are used to justify hostility and prejudice.

3. Dehumanization: People are judged based on their religion, caste, or community rather than their character or actions.

How to Overcome Divisions in God's Name

Recognize the Universal Essence of God, and understand that God, as the source of creation, transcends names, forms, and rituals. Focus on the universal principles of love, kindness, and harmony that every faith promotes. Celebrate diversity and appreciate the richness of various traditions and beliefs as expressions of humanity's creativity and connection to the divine. Learn from different faiths to deepen your understanding of spirituality.

Respect others' beliefs without judgment or the need to prove superiority. Approach differences with curiosity and an open heart, seeking to learn rather than criticize. Speak out against the use of religion or caste to justify discrimination, inequality, or violence. Advocate for inclusive practices that honour the spiritual worth of all individuals. Focus on love, service, and compassion as the true expressions of faith. Build bridges between communities through acts of kindness and shared goals.

Reclaiming God as a Unifying Force

God is not limited by human-made boundaries of caste, community, or region. When we see God in every living being, value humanity above rituals or labels, and act with love, empathy, and humility, we return to the universal truth of spirituality. The ultimate purpose of belief in God is not to divide but to unite, to inspire, and to uplift all beings. By embracing this higher understanding, humanity can transcend divisions and create a world of peace and harmony.

Contribution and Fulfilment –
The System Upgrade

XXVI

17. Beyond the Self: Finding Joy in Contribution

Contributions that bring peace, happiness, and a sense of fulfilment often align with personal values, create a positive impact, and foster deep connections with others. Here are some ways to contribute meaningfully to the world while nurturing your inner peace:

1. Acts of Kindness and Compassion

Helping those in need, assisting underprivileged individuals through donations, teaching, or volunteering at shelters or orphanages can bring immense satisfaction. Listening to others, being present, and genuinely listening to someone who needs support can create a profound connection and bring joy to both sides. Random Acts of Kindness such as small, thoughtful gestures like paying for someone's meal, writing a thank-you note, or helping a stranger can spread happiness.

2. Empowering Others

Sharing your knowledge and skills with those eager to learn be it children, students, or professionals can create a ripple effect of positive change. Uplifting women and marginalized groups by supporting individuals to achieve their potential through mentorship, funding, or advocacy adds meaning to your efforts. Creating Opportunities for helping someone start a career, learn a new skill, or build a business fosters both personal and community growth.

3. Connecting with Nature

Tree planting and rewilding, engaging in activities like planting trees, restoring habitats, or protecting biodiversity allows you to leave a legacy for future generations. Gardening and growing your own vegetables, herbs, or flowers connects you with nature while nurturing your mind. Spending Time Outdoors, and organizing clean-up drives for beaches, rivers, or forests can create a tangible impact and provide spiritual refreshment.

4. Sharing Your Creative Side

Writing or Storytelling, sharing your journey, experiences, or wisdom through blogs, books, or social media can inspire others while giving you a platform for expression. Art and Craft, creating and donating handmade items, like blankets for the homeless or art for a community centre, brings warmth and beauty to the world. Cooking for Others by preparing meals for friends, neighbours, or those in need is a gesture filled with love and care.

5. Supporting Causes You Believe In

Volunteering for a Cause; whether it's environmental conservation, education, or animal welfare, actively participating in causes that resonate with your values can be deeply fulfilling. Donating resources money, time, or expertise to organizations working for meaningful change provides satisfaction in knowing you've made a difference.

6. Building Strong Relationships

Strengthening Family Bonds, spending quality time with your loved ones, resolving conflicts, and creating joyful memories fosters a sense of belonging. Fostering the Community by organizing local events or simply being an active and supportive neighbour can strengthen your ties to the community.

7. Healing and Selfless Giving

Donating blood or organs and offering a part of yourself to save lives is one of the most profound ways to contribute. Supporting mental health and providing emotional support to those struggling with mental health issues helps create a safe and understanding world.

8. Spiritual Contributions

Meditation and prayer groups participating in or leading groups focused on mindfulness, gratitude, or spirituality spread peace and harmony. Charitable acts in faith following the teachings of your faith by serving others without expecting anything in return can be immensely rewarding.

9. Passing on Values

Inspiring the next generation by teaching children and young people the importance of kindness, responsibility, and empathy ensures your values live on. Write a memoir, fund a library, or support a school, leaving behind something meaningful for the future.

10. Loving Yourself and Others

Practicing self-love by taking care of your mental, physical, and emotional well-being allows you to contribute to the world as your best self. Spreading positivity by smiling, encouraging, and uplifting others creates a ripple effect of happiness.

Contributions that align with your purpose and values not only make the world a better place but also fill your heart with peace and fulfilment. When you see the positive outcomes of your actions whether it's a smile, a greener world, or a person empowered you feel deeply connected to life and its higher meaning.

XXVII

18. Creating a Ripple Effect

The ripple effect of holistic health and happiness is profound and transformative, touching every aspect of your life and extending its influence into the universe around you. When you take charge of your physical, mental, emotional, and spiritual health, you begin to align with the natural harmony of existence, creating a life that is meaningful, joyful, and deeply fulfilling.

Physical Health: The Foundation of Vitality

Caring for your body through proper nutrition, exercise, and rest enhances your energy levels and overall resilience. Each small habit like choosing a wholesome meal, taking a mindful walk, or prioritizing sleep becomes a brick in the foundation of a vibrant life. This vitality spills into your environment, enabling you to engage with the world with vigour and positivity.

Mental Health: Cultivating Clarity and Focus

Mental well-being arises from habits that nurture your mind, such as practicing mindfulness, journaling, or learning something new. These habits strengthen your ability to focus, solve problems, and remain calm amidst challenges. A healthy mind radiates clarity and creativity, inspiring those around you and fostering a sense of collective growth.

Emotional Health: The Power of Connection

Emotional health blossoms when you embrace self-awareness, practice gratitude, and build meaningful relationships. Small habits like expressing gratitude daily, acknowledging your emotions without judgment, and practicing forgiveness create waves of emotional resilience and harmony. When you are emotionally balanced, you become a source of comfort and inspiration for others, spreading kindness and understanding in your personal and professional circles.

Spiritual Health: Aligning with the Universe

Spiritual health connects you to the greater purpose of life and the infinite energy of the universe. Through practices like meditation, prayer, or simply spending time in nature, you attune yourself to a higher consciousness. This alignment helps you find meaning in every experience, no matter how small and fosters a sense of peace and interconnectedness. A spiritually fulfilled person radiates a sense of purpose that uplifts not only themselves but also those around them.

The Ripple Effect on Life and the Universe

When you commit to improving your holistic health, the benefits extend far beyond you. The happiness and energy you cultivate influence your family, friends, and community, inspiring them to prioritize their well-being. This ripple effect builds a network of positivity and resilience, creating a collective energy that uplifts society.

As your inner world transforms, so does your outer world. You start to notice the beauty in everyday moments, the interconnectedness of life, and the harmony in the universe. Each small habit whether it's a morning stretch, a few moments of gratitude, or a mindful meal becomes a sacred act that aligns you with the heaven of the universe.

Holistic health is not just a personal journey; it's a universal vibration. When you nurture your physical, mental, emotional, and spiritual well-being, you harmonize with the rhythm of life itself. This alignment creates meaning, joy, and fulfilment, not just for you but for everything and everyone you touch. In this way, holistic health and happiness ripple outward, reminding us that we are all interconnected, and through self-care, we care for the universe.

Creating Heaven on Earth Through Small Habits

The beauty of holistic health lies in its accessibility. You don't need grand gestures or radical transformations to create lasting change. It begins with the smallest actions, done consistently. Drinking water mindfully, pausing to breathe deeply during stressful moments, taking time to stretch and move your body, or setting aside a few minutes each day to meditate each habit plants a seed of harmony within you.

Over time, these seeds grow into a garden of well-being, influencing your outlook, relationships, and contributions to the world. Your physical strength becomes a vessel for meaningful actions. Your mental clarity allows you to solve problems and make decisions with ease. Your emotional balance enables you to approach others with compassion, and your spiritual connection helps you find purpose and joy in even the simplest moments.

As these habits become second nature, they create a sense of alignment that resonates deeply with the rhythm of the universe. This alignment isn't just about individual happiness; it's a profound shift in how you perceive and interact with the world. You begin to see how your choices, energy, and actions impact the collective consciousness.

The Universe Reflects Your Inner World

When you nurture your inner self, the universe responds. You may notice how your relationships deepen as you become more present and emotionally attuned. Your work becomes more fulfilling as you bring a sense of purpose and creativity to it. Even the mundane tasks of daily life take on a new sense of meaning, as they become acts of gratitude and mindfulness.

This shift doesn't just affect those immediately around you, it reverberates outward. Just as a single pebble dropped into a pond creates ripples that expand endlessly, your health and happiness send waves of positivity into the world. People who encounter your energy are inspired to seek their balance and well-being. This chain reaction creates a collective awakening, reminding humanity of its interconnectedness and shared responsibility for the health of the planet.

Living in the Heaven of the Universe

When you embrace holistic health, you align yourself with the natural flow of life, and this alignment creates a state of heaven on earth. This "heaven" isn't a distant, abstract concept it's a tangible experience of living fully in the present, connected to yourself, others, and the universe.

Every moment becomes sacred. Every interaction holds the potential for growth and love. Every challenge becomes an opportunity to deepen your connection with the infinite wisdom of life. By taking charge of your physical, mental, emotional, and spiritual well-being, you unlock a life of profound meaning, fulfilment, and joy.

In the end, the ripple effect of your journey transforms not only your life but also the lives of countless others, creating a universe that reflects the light and harmony within you. The key is understanding that every small habit matters, for it, is through these tiny, consistent actions that we build a heaven that is not separate from us but lives within us and radiates outward to touch the cosmos.

Ripples of Negativity

The ripple effect of negative choices and destructive emotions is the mirror opposite of the harmony that comes with holistic health and happiness. It creates an inner and outer reality that feels like hell a state of turmoil, misery, and disconnection that radiates outward, impacting not only your life but also the lives of those around you.

Physical Neglect: The First Domino

When you make poor choices for your physical health consuming harmful substances, neglecting exercise, or ignoring the needs of your body you set the stage for decay. Over time, these small, negative habits erode your energy and vitality, leaving you feeling sluggish, unwell, and disconnected from life. This neglect of the body acts as a gateway, amplifying emotional and mental struggles, and creating a vicious cycle that is difficult to break.

Mental Chaos: The Breeding Ground of Hatred and Jealousy

A neglected mind becomes a breeding ground for negative thoughts, such as hatred, jealousy, and despair. When you allow these thoughts to dominate, your perspective on life becomes skewed. Instead of seeing growth opportunities, you focus on what others have that you don't, leading to resentment and bitterness. This mental chaos isolates you, making it harder to connect authentically with others or even recognize your worth.

Emotional Wounds: Carrying the Past Like Chains

When your heart holds onto wounds whether they stem from betrayal, failure, or personal insecurities you begin to perceive the world through a lens of pain. This emotional baggage becomes the fuel for actions rooted in revenge, malice, and victimhood. Instead of healing, you replay old hurts, projecting them onto others. You may even create chaos in others' lives, attempting to drag them down to your level, thinking that it will ease your suffering. But the truth is, each act of destruction only deepens the wound within you.

Spiritual Disconnect: A Hollow Existence

In this state, your spirit becomes disconnected from the greater meaning of life. You lose sight of the beauty, interconnectedness, and infinite possibilities that surround you. Externally, you might appear to have everything success, relationships, or material wealth but internally, there is nothing but emptiness. The spiritual void leaves you restless, searching for fulfilment in ways that only perpetuate your suffering.

The Ripple Effect of Destruction

The negativity you cultivate within yourself doesn't stay contained; it spreads. Your interactions become tinged with anger, bitterness, or manipulation, causing harm to your relationships. The chaos you create in others' lives might temporarily give you a sense of power or satisfaction, but it ultimately leaves you more isolated and miserable. The pain you inflict on others reflects on you, reinforcing the hell you've built for yourself.

Even worse, this ripple effect doesn't stop with you. Your negativity influences the energy around you, affecting your family, friends, and community. It becomes a cycle of destruction, where those around you may also adopt toxic patterns, perpetuating the misery.

The Reality of Responsibility

At the core of this experience is a painful truth: the hell you experience is not about others, situations, or external events. It reflects what's in your heart. If your heart is filled with hatred, jealousy, and agony, that is the world you will see and create. No matter how much you blame others or external circumstances, the reality of your suffering comes from within.

When you try to pull someone else down out of jealousy, revenge, or anger you only harm yourself. The energy you expend to destroy others never brings true satisfaction, because it disconnects you further from your well-being and purpose. You may succeed in creating chaos in others' lives, but the chaos within you will only grow, leaving you trapped in a cycle of misery.

Hell in the Universe: A Self-Created Prison

Hell in the universe is not a place; it is a state of being. It is the torment of living with unresolved pain, unhealed wounds, and a disconnection from your true self. When your actions are driven by negativity and your heart clings to grudges, you are imprisoned by your own choices. The outer appearance of success, power, or control cannot mask the inner emptiness, for true peace and happiness cannot coexist with hatred and jealousy.

The Way Out

The only way to break free from this ripple of destruction is to take responsibility for your inner world. Healing begins when you stop blaming others, let go of grudges, and turn inward to address the pain in your heart. By cultivating compassion, forgiveness, and self-love, you can reverse the cycle and begin creating ripples of positivity instead of destruction. It is a challenging journey, but one that leads to freedom, fulfilment, and reconnection with the harmony of the universe. In the end, the hell you experience is a mirror of your inner state. The choice to remain in it or to rise above it is yours and it starts with the courage to confront and heal your own heart.

XXVIII

19. Designing a Legacy of Love and Purpose

Loving Others Without Judgment: A Path to True Compassion

Loving others without judgment is a profound spiritual practice that allows us to connect deeply with humanity and foster a world of understanding and compassion. It requires us to see others as reflections of ourselves and approach them with an open heart and mind.

Understanding Love Beyond Judgment

Judgment often stems from our own insecurities, biases, or limited perspectives. True love transcends these barriers, focusing instead on acceptance by embracing others as they are, without the need to change or "fix" them. Seeing shared humanity in every person, regardless of differences in appearance, behaviour, or beliefs. Recognizing that everyone is shaped by their unique experiences, just as we are. To love without judgment is to offer unconditional support and understanding, creating a safe space for others to be their authentic selves.

Practicing Love by Seeing Ourselves in Others' Shoes

The ability to see ourselves in another person's position is the cornerstone of empathy and non-judgmental love. Here's how we can cultivate this perspective:

1. Acknowledge Shared Humanity

Understand that all humans experience joy, pain, fear, and hope. These emotions unite us, regardless of external differences. Remind yourself that, like you, others are navigating life's challenges, seeking happiness, and dealing with their struggles.

2. Listen Without Bias

Truly hear others' stories, perspectives, and emotions without interrupting or forming judgments. Focus on understanding their feelings rather than forming a response or critique.

3. Assume Positive Intent

Believe that most people act with good intentions, even if their actions or words may seem flawed or hurtful. Recognize that misunderstandings often arise from pain, fear, or unmet needs, not malice.

4. Reflect on Your Own Imperfections

Accept your own shortcomings and past mistakes. When you recognize your fallibility, it becomes easier to extend the same understanding to others. Ask yourself, "How would I want to be treated if I were in their place?"

5. Imagine Their Perspective

Picture what it might feel like to live their life, face their challenges, and experience their emotions. This practice of mentally stepping into their shoes builds compassion and reduces judgment.

6. Let Go of Ego

Recognize that the need to judge often stems from ego a desire to feel superior or in control. Shift your focus from comparison to connection, valuing others' journeys as much as your own.

The Power of Loving Others Without Judgment

When you love others without judgment, your acceptance and understanding can help others overcome shame, guilt, or fear. People feel safe to open up and share their true selves, deepening relationships. Non-judgmental love encourages others to reflect, grow, and become their best selves.

Practical Steps to Love Others Unconditionally

1. Practice Patience: Allow people the time and space to express themselves fully without rushing to conclusions.

2. Cultivate Kindness: Speak and act with kindness, even in challenging situations. A gentle approach fosters mutual respect.

3. Release Expectations: Let go of rigid expectations about how others "should" act or feel. Accept them as they are.

4. Express Gratitude: Appreciate the unique qualities and contributions of others. Focus on their strengths rather than their flaws.

5. Seek Common Ground: Focus on shared values and experiences rather than differences, building bridges of understanding.

Loving Through Empathy and Compassion

Empathy is the foundation of unconditional love. When you see others through the lens of their experiences. You no longer view their mistakes as failures but as lessons on their journey. You recognize that their pain might manifest in ways that seem difficult, yet it reflects their need for love and healing. You connect with their humanity, understanding that their joys and struggles mirror your own.

The Ripple Effect of Non-Judgmental Love

Loving others without judgment has a transformative impact. It brings inner peace and fulfilment, freeing you from the negativity of judgment. It creates a safe and nurturing environment for people to grow and thrive. Acts of unconditional love inspire kindness, empathy, and harmony in communities and beyond.

To love others without judgment is to embrace their humanity as your own. By seeing yourself in their shoes, you develop a deeper understanding of their struggles, joys, and individuality. This practice not only enriches your relationships but also aligns you with the universal essence of a loved one that uplifts, heals, and unites all beings.

My Husband – The True Legacy of My Life

In the tapestry of my life, my husband is the most vibrant and steadfast thread. His unwavering love, progressive outlook, and relentless support have shaped my journey, both personally and professionally.

Our story began as two hearts nurturing each other's dreams. Leaving my PhD in nano-biotechnology to focus on our marriage and family was a daunting choice, but he ensured I never saw it as a compromise. He reminded me that growth and learning come in many forms and supported my pursuit of knowledge through online courses and distance education.

Unlike many, he celebrates my success as his own. From applauding my small victories to encouraging my aspirations, he has been my cheerleader and guide. His progressive mindset uncommon in a world of rigid gender roles has allowed me to thrive as an individual, not just as a wife or mother.

Together, we've built a beautiful family. Our children, with their independent spirits and resilience, reflect the best of us. His pride in them and his love for me create a home filled with encouragement and joy.

Life hasn't been without challenges, but his unwavering presence has been my backbone. Whether managing our children while I pursued my goals or offering words of comfort during setbacks, he has shown me the true meaning of partnership. It's not about grand gestures but showing up every day with love and support.

In quiet moments, we reflect on our journey, our sacrifices, joys, and lessons. His optimism transforms challenges into opportunities, teaching me that growth is as much about effort as it is about outcomes.

He redefines what it means to be a man and partner, championing equality and shared growth. Through his example, our children are learning kindness, determination, and mutual respect. I am comforted knowing they will carry these values forward.

Looking ahead, I feel immense gratitude. While there's still so much, I want to achieve, I know he'll be there, cheering me on, as he always has. Our marriage is beautifully imperfect, filled with laughter, growth, and resilience.

He is not just my husband but my partner, my anchor, and my inspiration. With him, life feels fuller, dreams feel closer, and love feels endless. For all that he is and all that we share, I am eternally grateful.

ಶ್ರೀ

XXIX

20.Epilogue – The Journey to Wholeness

The Journey of Wholeness

The title "Epilogue: The Journey of Wholeness" symbolizes the culmination of a profound transformation. It reflects the essence of closing one chapter of struggle, confusion, or misalignment and embracing a new beginning rooted in harmony and intentionality. This journey is not just about external achievements but a deeply personal alignment of the mind, body, and soul a holistic integration of oneself with their true purpose.

The journey begins with the mind, the foundation of all human experiences. When your thoughts align with your life's intentions, a powerful chain reaction is set into motion. Your thoughts dictate your behaviour, which then shapes your actions. Repeatedly, these actions form habits that mould your lifestyle.

A lifestyle anchored in conscious alignment brings peace, contentment, and clarity. However, when the mind is scattered or influenced by external chaos, life veers off course. The misalignment creates a dissonance between your desires and reality, leading to regret, self-doubt, and even resentment toward yourself and others.

The mind is the key to unlocking holistic health not just for you but for the relationships and love that surround you. A centred mind cultivates self-awareness and balance, which ripples into every aspect of life, from personal well-being to family harmony. Your ability to perceive, respond, and thrive depends on the clarity and perspective of your mind.

This epilogue is about closing the chapters of restlessness, external dependency, and inner chaos, and opening a new chapter of intentional living. It invites you to take control, honour your mind's power, and embrace a lifestyle that resonates with your authentic self. In doing so, you create a life of wholeness a journey of self-discovery, healing, and profound joy shared with those you love.

The journey of wholeness is not a destination but a continuous process of learning, evolving, and reconnecting with your inner self. It requires a conscious effort to unlearn the patterns that no longer serve you and replace them with habits that align with your highest potential. This is not easy, as the external environment often pulls you in conflicting directions, clouding your sense of self and purpose. However, when you take ownership of your mind, you reclaim your power to navigate life with intention and grace.

At the heart of this journey lies mindfulness the ability to observe your thoughts without judgment, to understand their origins, and to guide them with purpose. Mindfulness allows you to break free from reactive patterns and choose responses that nurture your well-being. It helps you bridge the gap between who you are and who you aspire to be, paving the way for authenticity.

As your mind becomes more aligned, the effects ripple outward. Your relationships flourish as you begin to see others with compassion rather than through the lens of your unresolved frustrations. You find joy in the simple moments of life and a deeper connection with your loved ones. Your career, passions, and personal growth become expressions of your inner peace, rather than desperate attempts to seek validation or escape dissatisfaction.

This epilogue also acknowledges that setbacks are part of the journey. Wholeness is not about perfection but about resilience the ability to realign after every misstep, to forgive yourself, and to keep moving forward with hope and determination. Each challenge you face is an opportunity to grow stronger and more self-aware, turning pain into wisdom and struggle into strength.

Ultimately, "Epilogue: The Journey of Wholeness" is a call to action. It invites you to take responsibility for your life by first taking responsibility for your mind. It reminds you that everything you seek peace, love, and fulfilment starts from within. By committing to this journey, you don't just change your life; you transform the lives of those around you, creating a ripple effect of positivity and purpose.

Wholeness is a journey of embracing yourself fully, imperfections and all, and living each day with intention, authenticity, and love. It is the most profound gift you can give to yourself and the world.

XXX

Interactive Elements

Here are some templates to help you connect with your true self, purpose, and happiness:

Template 1: Discovering Your Values and Beliefs

1. What is most important to me in life? (e.g., family, relationships, personal growth, creativity)

2. What do I stand for? (e.g., honesty, kindness, fairness, compassion)

3. What do I believe about myself and the world? (e.g., optimistic, pessimistic, hopeful, cynical)

4. How do my values, beliefs, and principles align with my current life and goals?

Template 2: Exploring Your Passions and Interests

1. What activities make me feel most alive and engaged? (e.g., hobbies, creative pursuits, sports, volunteering)

2. What topics do I enjoy learning about and exploring? (e.g., science, history, art, philosophy)

3. What kind of work or activities would I do if I didn't have to worry about money or practicality?

4. How can I incorporate more of my passions and interests into my daily life?

Template 3: Identifying Your Strengths and Talents

1. What are my natural strengths and talents? (e.g., problem-solving, communication, leadership, creativity)

2. What skills have I developed over time? (e.g., language proficiency, musical ability, athletic prowess)

3. What kind of feedback do I receive from others about my strengths and talents?

4. How can I use my strengths and talents to make a positive impact in the world?

Template 4: Envisioning Your Ideal Life

1. What does my ideal life look like? (e.g., career, relationships, living situation, personal growth)

2. What kind of work or activities would I be doing in my ideal life?

3. What kind of relationships would I have in my ideal life? (e.g., romantic, friendships, family)

4. What kind of personal growth and development would I be experiencing in my ideal life?

Template 5: Creating a Personal Mission Statement

1. What is my purpose or mission in life? (e.g., to help others, to create something meaningful, to inspire and educate)

2. What kind of impact do I want to make in the world?

3. What kind of person do I want to be? (e.g., kind, compassionate, honest, courageous)

4. What kind of legacy do I want to leave behind?

Template 6: Practicing Self-Reflection and Journaling

1. What am I grateful for today? (e.g., relationships, health, personal growth)

2. What am I proud of accomplishing? (e.g., work, personal projects, relationships)

3. What am I struggling with or challenged by? (e.g., work, relationships, personal growth)

4. What can I learn from my experiences and challenges?

Template 7: Cultivating Mindfulness and Presence

1. What are my thoughts and feelings in this present moment?

2. What sensations am I experiencing in my body? (e.g., tension, relaxation, pain, pleasure)

3. What am I grateful for in this present moment?

4. What can I let go of or release in this present moment? (e.g., worries, fears, doubts)

XXXI

"Acts of Contribution" checklist

Contributing to the environment and making the world a better place involves a variety of actions that can collectively create a significant positive impact. Here are several ways individuals can contribute, categorized into environmental, societal, and personal efforts:

1. Environmental Contributions

A. Reducing Waste

Adopt zero-waste practices use reusable bags, bottles, and containers to minimize single-use plastics. Compost by turning organic waste into nutrient-rich soil, reducing landfill contributions. Recycle and upcycle properly segregate recyclables and creatively repurpose items to extend their lifecycle.

B. Conserving Energy and Resources

Save water, fix leaks, use water-efficient appliances, and adopt habits like turning off taps when not in use. Switch to Renewable Energy install solar panels or support green energy initiatives. Use energy-saving bulbs, insulate your home, and unplug devices when not in use.

C. Sustainable Transportation

Carpool or use public transport to reduce carbon emissions by sharing rides or using buses and trains. Use cycle or walk for non-polluting modes of transport when possible. Support electric vehicles transition to EVs if feasible, or support infrastructure development for cleaner transport.

D. Protecting Natural Ecosystems

Plant trees that combat climate change by absorbing CO2, providing oxygen, and supporting biodiversity. Protect wildlife avoid products contributing to habitat destruction and support conservation organizations. Support sustainable agriculture by buying from eco-friendly farms practicing regenerative farming techniques.

2. Societal Contributions

A. Advocacy and Education

Raise Awareness use social media platforms or community events to spread awareness about environmental issues. Support Legislation advocates for policies promoting renewable energy, pollution control, and conservation efforts. Volunteer by joining local clean-up drives, tree plantation campaigns, or organizations working on sustainability.

B. Support Local Communities

Buy local, and support small businesses and farmers who follow sustainable practices, reducing transportation emissions. Fairtrade products choose goods made ethically, ensuring fair wages and environmental care. Help vulnerable populations engage in initiatives like disaster relief, education drives, or providing essentials to underprivileged communities.

3. Personal Contributions

A. Mindful Consumption

Minimalism focuses on needs rather than wants to reduce unnecessary production and waste. Buy clothes from brands focusing on eco-friendly practices or thrift items instead of buying new ones.

B. Lifestyle Changes

A plant-based diet reduces meat consumption to lower your carbon and water footprint. Grow your food and cultivate a garden to reduce dependence on industrially produced food. Eco-friendly products choose biodegradable, toxin-free, and cruelty-free products for personal and home use.

4. Technological and Creative Innovations

Support green technology and invest in or promote technologies like solar batteries, wind turbines, or biodegradable materials. Innovate for sustainability, if skilled, design tools or systems that help combat environmental issues. Collaborate with startups partner with or support companies working toward environmental solutions.

5. Holistic Community Involvement

Educate the youth teach children about sustainability and involve them in eco-friendly practices from a young age. Create community gardens to encourage communal efforts to grow food and green urban spaces. Share resources, organize libraries, tool-sharing systems, or clothing swaps to reduce overconsumption.

By integrating these practices into daily life, supporting broader community efforts, and advocating for systemic change, individuals can contribute to a healthier planet and a more equitable world. Each action, no matter how small, creates ripples that collectively bring about transformative change.

XXXII
Additional Resources

The Cognitive Dysfunction of a Family Cult: The Silent Impact of Gaslighting

Family is often seen as the cornerstone of emotional stability and growth. However, when a family operates under a dysfunctional framework, especially one resembling a cult-like dynamic, the repercussions on an individual's cognitive and emotional well-being can be profound. At the heart of this dysfunction lies gaslighting a manipulative tactic that distorts reality and erodes the victim's sense of self.

The Cult-Like Family Dynamic

In a family cult, one or more members take on authoritarian roles, often demanding absolute loyalty and obedience. The environment is rigid, with unwritten rules that dictate behaviour, beliefs, and relationships. Dissent is not tolerated; individuality is stifled in Favor of conformity.

Such families often create an "us vs. them" mentality, isolating members from external perspectives. Emotional manipulation, guilt, and fear are used to maintain control, leaving little room for trust or genuine emotional connection. In this oppressive atmosphere, gaslighting becomes a tool of choice.

Gaslighting: The Invisible Poison

Gaslighting in a family setting involves consistently denying a member's perceptions, experiences, or emotions. Phrases like, "You're imagining things," "You're too sensitive," or "That never happened," are common. Over time, this tactic creates self-doubt, confusion, and dependency. The victim begins to question their own reality, making them more susceptible to control.

How Gaslighting Affects the Brain

1. Chronic Stress and the Brain:

Gaslighting triggers chronic stress, releasing a flood of cortisol into the brain. Over time, this can shrink the hippocampus, the region responsible for memory and learning, and enlarge the amygdala, the brain's fear center. This structural change makes it harder to process emotions, recall events accurately, and think critically.

2. Impaired Emotional Regulation:

Victims of gaslighting struggle with emotional regulation. The constant invalidation of their feelings leads to heightened anxiety and depression. The brain's prefrontal cortex, responsible for decision-making and self-control, becomes less effective, leaving the individual vulnerable to further manipulation.

3. Cognitive Dissonance:

Gaslighting creates a disconnect between what the victim knows to be true and what they are being told. This cognitive dissonance forces the brain into a state of mental conflict, requiring immense energy to reconcile the disparity. Over time, this mental exhaustion diminishes problem-solving abilities and reduces resilience.

4. Erosion of Identity:

By undermining a person's sense of reality, gaslighting dismantles their identity. The victim becomes dependent on the manipulator for validation and direction, losing their sense of autonomy.

Breaking Free: The Path to Healing

Recovering from a cognitively dysfunctional family cult begins with recognizing the patterns of gaslighting. Therapy, journaling, and rebuilding connections with supportive individuals can help restore a sense of self.

1. Validation of Reality:

Acknowledging and validating one's own experiences is the first step toward healing. This often involves confronting painful truths and rewriting the narrative imposed by the family.

2. Rebuilding Neural Pathways:

Mindfulness practices, such as meditation and grounding techniques, can help repair the brain's stress response. Cognitive-behavioral therapy (CBT) is particularly effective in challenging distorted beliefs and developing healthier thought patterns.

3. Establishing Boundaries:

Setting firm boundaries with toxic family members is essential. This might mean limiting contact or, in extreme cases, cutting ties altogether.

4. Cultivating a Support Network:

Reaching out to trusted friends, support groups, or mental health professionals can provide the external perspective and encouragement needed for recovery.

Key Insight

The impact of gaslighting in a cognitively dysfunctional family cult is not merely emotional; it rewires the brain in ways that can have lasting effects. Yet, the human brain is remarkably resilient. With self-awareness, therapy, and support, it is possible to reclaim one's reality, rebuild self-trust, and break free from the chains of manipulation. The journey may be long, but the destination a life of authenticity and freedom is worth every step.

Healing from the Chaos of Self-Absorbed Individuals

1. Opening: Setting the Scene

In every family or close-knit group, there's often someone who thrives on attention, disrupts the peace, and portrays themselves as a victim when challenged. At first, their behaviour seems harmless, perhaps even charming. But over time, a toxic pattern emerges love-bombing, manipulation, and emotional abuse. This was my reality a confusing, frustrating storm that tested my peace and spirit.

2. The Emotional Impact of Toxic Relationships

Navigating relationships with self-absorbed individuals is exhausting. They demand constant attention and validation, manipulating others into their emotional drama. Their actions seemingly minor at first slowly corrode your sense of self. They'll lavish you with affection one moment and undermine you the next. Their ability to charm others while isolating you leaves you questioning your worth and sanity.

For me, the constant emotional landmines took a toll. I doubted myself, wondering if I was the problem. The betrayal felt personal, yet their actions reflected their insecurities, not my values. Still, the pain was real, and the confusion cut deep.

3. Your Turning Point

The moment of clarity came when I realized I could no longer sacrifice my peace for someone who thrived on my pain. Their chaos, though painful, had fertilized my spirit. It taught me resilience and the importance of self-love. I began to see their behaviour for what it was: a cycle I didn't have to be part of. I decided to reclaim my happiness and rebuild my boundaries.

4. Wisdom and Lessons Learned

Happiness is Internal: I discovered that true happiness is a flame you nurture within. It isn't dependent on external validation or someone else's approval.

Set Boundaries Without Guilt: Protecting your peace isn't selfish; it's survival. Saying "no" is an act of self-respect and self-care.

Recognize Manipulation: Self-absorbed individuals are often skilled at love-bombing and playing the victim. Learn to identify these patterns and detach them emotionally.

Healing is a journey: Healing from emotional abuse isn't linear. Some days will feel empowering, while others might be filled with doubt. But each step forward strengthens your spirit.

5. To Stay or Let Go?

One of the hardest decisions is whether to maintain a relationship with someone toxic, especially when they're family. Walking away isn't easy, but sometimes it's the most loving choice you can make for yourself. Family is about love, respect, and support not enduring abuse. Letting go isn't abandoning; it's prioritizing your well-being.

6. Empower and Inspire

Healing from someone's chaos isn't easy, but it's possible. Each step away from their influence brings you closer to your authentic self. Remember, your spirit is stronger than your storm. Protect your peace, nurture your happiness, and trust in your resilience. You deserve a life free from manipulation and filled with self-love and genuine connections.

Addressing Emotional Abuse

This piece offers a strong foundation for addressing emotional abuse and gaslighting, particularly in relationships with self-absorbed individuals. Here are some suggestions to refine and enhance the content:

1. Clarify the Effects of Emotional Abuse and Gaslighting

- Expand on how gaslighting specifically undermines one's confidence and perception of reality. This could include phrases like:

"Gaslighting can make you question your intuition and memory, leaving you in a state of self-doubt and dependency."

- Including an example (real or hypothetical) can make this section more relatable.

2. Deepen the Turning Point

- Elaborate on how you recognized the patterns of manipulation and emotional abuse. For instance:

"I started noticing inconsistencies between their words and actions, and the repetitive cycle of idealization, devaluation, and discarding."

- Reflecting on the emotions during this realization could add depth.

3. Actionable Wisdom and Tools for Healing

- Suggest specific practices like journaling, seeking therapy, or joining support groups to aid healing.

"Journaling allowed me to untangle my emotions and see the patterns of manipulation."

4. Strengthen the Empowerment Message

- Add affirmations or motivational lines to encourage readers in their healing journey. For instance:

"You are not what happened to you; you are who you choose to become after it."

5. Balance with Personal Touch

- While the narrative is impactful, including more personal anecdotes could make it even more authentic.

"I remember a specific moment when they dismissed my feelings as 'overreacting,' and that small instance opened my eyes to years of subtle manipulation."

ॐ

XXXIII

Templates and Worksheets

Here are some templates to help you identify toxic traits, feel safe and secure in relationships, and recognize signs of self-doubt and gaslighting:

Template 1: Identifying Toxic Traits in Yourself and Others

1. Manipulation:

Do you or the other person use guilt, anger, or self-pity to control others?

Are you or the other person prone to lying, hiding the truth, or distorting reality?

2. Emotional Unavailability:

Do you or the other person have difficulty expressing emotions or intimacy?

Are you or the other person prone to withdrawing or becoming distant when emotional issues arise?

3. Gaslighting:

Do you or the other person deny or distort reality to manipulate others?

Are you or the other person prone to making others question their own sanity or memory?

4. Self-Centeredness:

Do you or the other person prioritize your own needs and desires over others' feelings and well-being?

Are you or the other person prone to taking credit for others' work or ideas?

5. Disrespect and Condescension:

Do you or the other person frequently criticize, belittle, or mock others?

Are you or the other person prone to talking down to others or acting superior?

Template 2: Feeling Safe and Secure in Relationships

1. Communication:

Do you feel heard and understood by the other person?

Are you able to express your thoughts and feelings without fear of judgment or rejection?

2. Trust:

Do you trust the other person to be honest and transparent with you?

Are you able to rely on the other person to follow through on commitments and maintain boundaries?

3. Emotional Support:

Does the other person offer emotional support and validation when you need it?

Are you able to provide emotional support and validation to the other person in return?

4. Respect and Boundaries:

Does the other person respect your boundaries and personal space?

Are you able to maintain healthy boundaries and communicate your needs clearly to the other person?

5. Consistency and Reliability:

Does the other person consistently show up and follow through on commitments?

Are you able to rely on the other person to be consistent and dependable?

Template 3: Recognizing Signs of Self-Doubt and Gaslighting

1. Self-Doubt:

Do you frequently question your own judgment, memory, or perceptions?

Do you feel uncertain or insecure about your decisions or actions?

2. Gaslighting:

Does the other person deny or distort reality to manipulate you?

Do you feel like you're going crazy or questioning your own sanity?

3. Emotional Manipulation:

Does the other person use guilt, anger, or self-pity to control you?

Do you feel like you're walking on eggshells around the other person?

4. Dismissing or Minimizing:

Does the other person dismiss or minimize your feelings or experiences?

Do you feel like your emotions or concerns are not being taken seriously?

Template 4: Evaluating Your Attachment Style

1. Secure Attachment:

Do you feel comfortable with intimacy and emotional closeness?

Are you able to maintain a sense of independence and autonomy in your relationships?

2. Anxious-Preoccupied Attachment:

Do you frequently worry about rejection or abandonment?

Are you overly dependent on your partner or others for emotional validation?

3. Dismissive-Avoidant Attachment:

Do you tend to avoid intimacy and emotional closeness?

Are you uncomfortable with vulnerability and emotional expression?

4. Fearful-Avoidant Attachment:

Do you fear rejection and abandonment, but also struggle with intimacy and emotional closeness?

Are you prone to sabotaging relationships or pushing partners away?

Template 5: Recognizing Signs of Over-Attachment

1. Over-Dependence:

Do you feel like you can't function or make decisions without your partner?

Are you overly reliant on your partner for emotional validation and support?

2. Loss of Identity:

Have you lost touch with your own interests, hobbies, and passions?

Do you feel like you're losing yourself in the relationship?

3. Sacrificing Own Needs:

Are you consistently sacrificing your own needs and desires to accommodate your partner?

Do you feel resentful or bitter about the sacrifices you're making?

4. Ignoring Red Flags:

Are you ignoring or downplaying red flags or warning signs in the relationship?

Do you feel like you're staying in the relationship despite your better judgment?

Designing Your Life With Alignment And Purpose

Life's Masterpiece: Crafting Your Own Story

Life's conclusion is not just an ending; it's the essence of how every fragment of your being comes together to create a personal masterpiece. This book serves as a guide to understanding that your happiness, fulfilment, and growth lie solely in your own hands. If you believe someone else holds the key to your joy, it's merely an illusion. The reality is that the responsibility for your life rests squarely with you.

The universe has gifted you a life brimming with potential and possibilities. How you shape it depends entirely on your choices. When your body, mind, heart, and soul align, they form the foundation for a life of balance and harmony. This alignment is the key to true happiness and personal growth.

Embracing Challenges and Heartbreak

Every heartbreak, challenge, and failure you face is a stepping stone to becoming a better version of yourself. These moments aren't obstacles; they're opportunities to learn, grow, and evolve. The book emphasizes the importance of embracing these experiences as vital parts of your journey. They are the universe's way of teaching resilience and helping you uncover your inner strength.

Unlearning and Openness

One of the book's core messages is the necessity of unlearning. We often hold onto perceptions, beliefs, and habits that no longer serve us. To truly grow, you must be open to change and ready to adapt to situations based on their demands rather than your emotions. While emotions can cloud judgment, adaptability, and awareness allow you to respond with clarity and purpose.

Rewriting Your Narrative

Life is not static, and neither should your story be. This book encourages you to keep rewriting your narrative. Clinging to outdated perceptions and stagnant beliefs leads to stagnation. Growth requires constant learning and the courage to redefine yourself as you move through life. When you stop learning, you become stuck, and the longer you remain in that state, the harder it is to break free.

Designing Your Life

You are invited to become the designer of your life. This isn't just about setting goals but aligning every aspect of your being to achieve them. Living intentionally, with purpose, means recognizing that every choice you make shapes your reality.

This book gently reminds you that life is inherently beautiful, even in its chaos. It's a call to take charge, embrace challenges, and grow with every experience. Your happiness, success, and growth are within your control. All it takes is taking responsibility, staying curious, and remaining open to the endless possibilities the universe offers.

This is more than a guide it's an empowerment tool, encouraging you to become the author of your life story. Life is what you make of it, and the pen is in your hands.

Appendices

Appendix A: Tools for Physical Health (Chapters 3-6)

- **Daily Rituals for Longevity:** Suggested habits such as exercise, balanced nutrition, and adequate sleep.
- **Weight Management Myths:** Common misconceptions debunked for sustainable health practices.

Appendix B: Tools for Mental Health (Chapters 7-10)

- **Grounding Techniques:** Methods like deep breathing and sensory focus to reduce anxiety.
- **Growth Mindsets:** Strategies to cultivate resilience and adaptability.

Appendix C: Techniques for Emotional Health (Chapters 11-13)

- **Emotional Signal Awareness:** Recognizing emotions as indicators of deeper needs.
- **Forgiveness Practices:** Steps to work through anger or resentment.

Appendix D: Practices for Spiritual Growth (Chapters 14-18)

- **Inner Peace Practices**: Meditation, prayer, and journaling exercises.
- **Interconnectedness Activities**: Exercises to reflect on unity with nature and humanity.

Appendix E: Self-Assessments and Templates (Chapters 30-33)

- **Checklists**: Tools for evaluating balance across the four health dimensions.
- **Reflection Prompts**: Guided questions for introspection after each chapter.
- **Worksheets**: Templates for goal setting, daily habits, and personal growth plans.

৪৩

APPENDICES